Improving Students' Writing, K-8

Improving Students' Writing, K-8

FROM MEANING-MAKING TO HIGH STAKES!

DIANE M. BARONE
JOAN TAYLOR

CORWIN PRESS
A SAGE Publications Company
Thousand Oaks, California

For information:

Corwin Press
A Sage Publications Company
2455 Teller Road
Thousand Oaks, California 91320
www.corwinpress.com

Sage Publications Ltd
1 Oliver's Yard
55 City Road
London EC1Y 1SP
United Kingdom

Sage Publications India Pvt. Ltd.
B-42, Panchsheel Enclave
Post Box 4109
New Delhi 110 017 India

Printed in the United States of America

Library of Congress Cataloging-in-Publication Data

Barone, Diane M.
Improving students' writing, K–8 : from meaning-making to high stakes! / Diane M. Barone and Joan Taylor.
    p. cm.
Includes bibliographical references and index.
ISBN 1-4129-1711-5 (cloth) — ISBN 1-4129-1712-3 (pbk.)
    1. English language—Composition and exercises—Study and teaching. I. Taylor, Joan. II. Title.
LB1576.B299 2006
372.62'3—dc22

                                                        2005008844

This book is printed on acid-free paper.

05   06   07   08   09   10   9   8   7   6   5   4   3   2   1

Acquisitions Editor:	Jean Ward
Editorial Assistant:	Jordan Barbakow
Production Editor:	Kristen Gibson
Copy Editor:	Barbara Coster
Typesetter:	C&M Digitals (P) Ltd.
Indexer:	John Hulse
Proofreader:	Kristin Bergstad
Cover Designer:	Rose Storey

Contents

Preface

Writing instruction is receiving renewed attention in policy circles as well as in state and local curriculum meetings because of new communication technologies and escalating assessment practices in schools. This book, filled with real-life vignettes, examples, and practical advice on writing instruction in K–8 classrooms, is meant for the teacher or soon-to-be teacher who is endeavoring to blend all the purposes and reasons for teaching writing into his or her instruction. This teacher sees writing instruction as more than preparation for national, state, or local assessment measures. He or she values multiple reasons for student writing that include having students use writing as a means of discovering, communicating, and demonstrating knowledge.

To help teachers understand the expectations for student writing today, we share historical perspectives throughout. This historical grounding allows teachers to see that many instructional practices and assessments have a rich history in American schools. Teachers become more aware of today's practices by understanding their historical roots.

In noting the importance of remembering past writing endeavors and using them to improve or understand current instruction, Graves (2004) wrote:

> Children want to write. These words are just as true now as they were 20 years ago when I first wrote them at the beginning of *Writing: Teachers and Children at Work* (1983). I would only add . . . if we let them. For the classroom environment has changed. Teachers are expected to teach twice as much curriculum within the same number of hours under the many number of classroom specialists. Time is in short supply—especially for writing. (p. 88)

Our book takes the words of Graves to heart and offers teachers ways to use writing to extend thinking and to develop the craft of writing. The craft of writing is important throughout the book, and we provide teachers with strategies to support the refinement of student writing.

Numerous examples are presented of young writers engaging in narrative, informational, descriptive, and persuasive texts with real purposes and audiences throughout the book. Reluctant writers, difficult writing situations, and various writing assessment formats are described, as is the use of writing as a window into a child's understanding of his or her intellectual and social self. Complementing the examples are real conversations shared between students and teachers so that readers can come to understand how teachers scaffold current student learning to more advanced knowledge in supportive ways. This book provides practical information to help teachers facilitate the writing development of all of their students.

Two of us have joined together to write this book. While we both have spent the majority of our careers as classroom teachers, each of us now has unique understandings and experiences that contribute to the strength and thoroughness of this book.

We first met, approximately 20 years ago, as classroom teachers at a summer institute for Northern Nevada Writing Project (a National Writing Project site). Diane was then embarking on the challenge of teaching a multiage classroom in a demonstration setting at the university while pursuing her doctoral degree. Her research has continued to focus on young children's literacy development, particularly in high poverty schools. Joan was a middle school teacher working on her master's degree and juggling a career and single parenthood. Her research has continued to focus on literacy instruction with an emphasis on writing.

We continued our friendship and collaboration intermittently over the years as Diane became a professor of literacy at the University of Nevada, Reno, and Joan worked as director of the Northern Nevada Writing Project and at the Nevada Department of Education as the state writing assessment consultant. Currently, we are both working on school reform issues in literacy within schools and among colleagues in Nevada.

We have organized this book to include both theoretical and practical considerations about writing instruction. Chapter 1 provides the foundation of the book with an exploration of writing to learn and understand. This chapter explores historical and current challenges to writing instruction. Literacy connections within a classroom that include speaking and writing, reading and writing, and finally listening/viewing and writing are described. The chapter ends with a discussion of the hardest parts of supporting student writers.

Chapter 2 builds from this base and moves to a consideration of writing to understand information. Readers might be surprised to see a chapter about informational writing precede discussion of narrative writing. We have placed this chapter purposely because we see informal and formal writing about content to be critical to student achievement in all subject areas. This chapter is organized around informal writing to learn and formal writing to learn. There is also discussion centered on the structure of informational text and helping students come to understand these structures and replicate them in their writing.

Chapter 3 moves from informational writing and reading to narrative writing. In this chapter we share overviews of the writing process and a writing workshop. Following this discussion is an exploration of writing development and gender differences in writing performance. As seen in Chapter 2, we explore informal and formal narrative writing.

Chapter 4 centers on writing as a craft. Within this chapter readers explore supporting students in their writing to real audiences and for real purposes. We also detail supporting students in revision and editing.

Chapter 5 looks deeply at assessment and preparing students for assessments. A historical perspective is shared about assessment methods so that readers understand today's concerns. Within the chapter, there are discussions centered on direct methods of assessment such as holistic scoring, primary trait scoring, multiple/analytic scoring, and portfolio assessments. The chapter includes pragmatic ways to support students in successfully responding to divergent and convergent writing assessment items.

Chapter 6, the final chapter in the book, is targeted to academic conversations that support students as they develop proficiency in writing. Many examples are showcased that allow teachers to view the subtleties within conversations that facilitate student writer development. Some of these conversations are informal and often occur during moments of teaching or transitions. Other conversations are more formal and occur during conferences or are written and targeted to student writing.

The focus of this book is supporting student writers from kindergarten through Grade 8. We recognize that it is the teacher who makes the difference in the writing experiences of students. The teacher is the only person who can create a classroom that nurtures student writers by providing numerous opportunities for supportive practice. It is our hope that this book serves teachers well as they strive to have all children become successful writers.

Corwin Press would like to thank the following reviewers for their contributions:

Kellie Riley Doubek
Instructional Technology and Literacy Consultant
Plainfield, Illinois

Joan Irwin
Vice President for Professional Development
The Peoples Publishing Group Inc.
Saddle Brook, New Jersey

Nancy McDonough
Second Grade Teacher
Tenafly, New Jersey

Anthony Mello, Ed.D.
Executive Director
New York ASCD

About the Authors

 **Diane M. Barone** is Professor of Literacy Studies at the University of Nevada, Reno. In her role at the university, she teaches courses in early literacy, diversity and literacy, and qualitative research. Her research interests center on young children, especially in high poverty schools, and how they develop in literacy. Her most current study followed 16 children from kindergarten through to Grade 6 to document their literacy growth.

She has been an editor of *Reading Research Quarterly* and has written numerous articles, book chapters, and books. Some of her recent books include *Reading First in the Classroom* with Joan Taylor and Darrin Hardman, *Literacy and Young Children: Research-Based Practices* with Lesley Morrow, *Teaching Early Literacy: Development, Assessment, and Instruction* with Marla Mallette and Shelley Xu, and *The National Board Certification Handbook*. She is also Principal Investigator for Reading First in Nevada and serves as a member of the board of the International Reading Association.

 **Joan Taylor** is a teacher-consultant who works with teachers and students in Title I schools in the Reno/Sparks area of Northern Nevada. She recently completed a dissertation on *A History of Written Composition Instruction in U.S. Elementary Schools*. Her research interests, in addition to historical and current perspectives on writing instruction, are focused on exploring teachers' stories on learning and teaching.

She has been a long-time middle school teacher in Washoe County Schools. She is also Nevada State Networks Writing Project Codirector, and during the past several years has authored a number of federally funded state literacy grants from the U.S. Department of Education totaling approximately $53 million. These include the Nevada Reading Excellence Act and Nevada Reading First grants.

1 Writing to Learn and Understand

Kennady looks furtively over her shoulder as she slips a note low and behind her to Alexis. As she props her book in front of her with one hand, she holds the paper patiently between her fingers in the other, waiting for Alexis to take it from her to pass to James and then on to Marissa as planned. Ms. Fletcher is busy at her desk, so unless she looks up or somebody acts suspicious, all will be well.

Good! Alexis has it. Now, on to James. He's such a dork! He'll probably read it, but who cares? It's not all that private. All Kennady really wants to know is if Marissa still plans on hanging out together after school.

Oh! Alexis has flipped it across the aisle to James. Only one more step to go. Kennady pretends to be reading her book, but she is scrutinizing James out of the corner of her eye. He is not passing the note.

Marissa is silently imploring James with her hand out, pointing at her palm, indicating she wants him to flick the message over to her. He, however, is enjoying all the interest he is receiving from the girls. As holder of this important missive, he has gained power and attention. He chuckles to himself as he slowly starts to unfold the note, enjoying the annoyed looks from Kennady and the insistent appeals from Marissa. Suddenly, he feels a thump at the back of his head. Diane, sitting immediately behind him, is warning him. Pass the note, or else!

James tosses the note and then turns around to face Diane, who is looking back at him innocently.

"James," calls out Ms. Fletcher. "Why aren't you reading? Turn around, take out a piece of paper, and write a brief essay on Why I Should Read During Free Reading Time."

The girls grin smugly at one another as James reluctantly complies.

H ow many countless classrooms have witnessed this same scenario? Generations worth. Students have seen writing as a form of social interchange as well as an instrument of discipline for countless years. Variations on the discipline approach include the forced essay that James encountered above as well as sentence writing, "I will not forget my homework" and also copying pages from the dictionary. (One of us still has 20 dictionary pages from *horse* to *insufferable* tucked away as a keepsake of just how insufferable she was as an eighth grader.)

There is some irony in punishing students with what we hope to instill in them as an intrinsically rewarding way of creating and communicating knowledge and understanding. The real purposes of writing in classrooms offer a variety of reasons to practice writing daily. Yes, that means every day.

Pulitzer Prize-winning journalist and writing teacher Donald Murray has a quote from Horace (65–8 B.C.) posted above his writing space that says *nulla dies sine linea*, which translated means, "Never a day without a line." This is a good motto for all writers, students and professionals alike.

PURPOSES FOR WRITING

The many purposes for writing are as varied as the many ways of thinking and communicating, and they sometimes overlap within a single piece of writing. Here is just a sampling, which we will expand upon later in this book.

1. *To learn.* The audience is usually the writer. Students take notes and draw diagrams and other graphics to make meaning of new concepts and ideas. Readers responding to this work can best help by asking questions and offering suggestions to make sure students are arriving at accurate information about concepts to form conclusions.

2. *To inform.* As in writing to learn, the audience is usually the writer but can also be the teacher or another reader-responder as a check on accurate understanding. By having students restate new information in their own words, the information takes on new meaning and awareness. Readers of this writing can best help by asking clarifying questions to make sure all the important details are included.

3. *To describe.* The audience for descriptive writing can vary with the overarching purposes of the piece. Students can describe processes, objects, and/or events in content areas, or with more personal narrative writing they can describe anything they want their audience to visualize from their

perspective. Readers can help by providing their interpretation of the description so writers can check for accuracy.

4. *To convince.* The audience is the person(s) targeted for influence. Sometimes the topic is a point of view and sometimes it is a specific action to be taken. Readers can help by questioning reasons, examples, and/or facts.

5. *To entertain.* Certainly, Kennady's note from the scenario at the beginning of this chapter was created to entertain. The audience is the intended recipient and the reader can respond best by being entertained.

6. *To connect new information to old ideas.* The audience can be the teacher but is more often the student. Making new subject matter personal by connecting it to established context is a way to learn and remember the new ideas and to know both old and new information in unique ways. The reader can respond best by asking comparison questions about both sets of information.

7. *To think about and revise ideas.* The audience is usually the writer but at some point can also be a peer editor. The reader can ask the writer for the kinds of feedback needed and then phrase responses based on those needs.

8. *To generalize.* The audience can be a teacher for evaluation or the writer to help solidify some specific details into a more general organization. Readers can best assist by asking questions about each category/ generalization to see if details fit.

9. *To analyze.* The audience is usually the teacher but can also be the writer. In examining details, that is, parts of the whole, the reader can help by making sure all the parts are defined and asking for information on why those parts are important.

10. *To clarify relationships.* The audience can be the teacher, a peer, or students themselves. The best way for the reader to offer response might be to restate a new understanding of the relationship based on information in the writing. Clarifying questions will also help, as might graphic organizers made by the reader in response to the writing.

11. *To explain simple to complex issues.* The audience can be another classmate or perhaps a younger student in a cross-peer tutoring situation. The best way this reader can provide response is to ask clarifying questions and to demonstrate understanding of the complex issue through summarizing or providing examples.

12. *To problem solve.* The audience is everyone engaged in the problem. Helpful response could include checking for strategies used and questions that deal with the process, problem, and possible/probable solutions.

13. *To problem find.* Looking at broad issues for problem formulation and solution can be aimed at a specific audience or simply for self. Students need to come up with their own problem-related questions, plans for answering those questions, and possible solutions. Donald Graves (2004) calls this "long thinking" (p. 167). The best response to this type of writing project could be, believe it or not, more questions.

14. *To make a request.* The audience is the person or entity to whom the request is being made. The best response is undoubtedly to grant the request; however, for a peer reviewer who is taking the role of the reader, the most helpful response would be to play devil's advocate and point out any flaws in logic or reasoning.

15. *To remember.* The audience is usually the writer himself or herself, and the best response is to recall information or ideas. This can also, however, apply to memoirs. The reader and writer connect an experience or memory, and the reader can relate what he or she believes the piece is describing or relating. The writer then can check for accuracy of message.

16. *To reflect.* This is usually focused on self-expression as well. A responder can ask for details or clarification to help the writer dig more deeply into a reflective piece of writing.

17. *To demonstrate knowledge and understanding.* The audience is usually someone in authority. It is designed to assess how well students understand information and/or concepts. Chapter 5 will deal with how to assist students in preparing for this type of writing task.

18. *To get better at writing.* The audience can vary, as can the formats. Like any craft, the more writing is practiced, the easier it becomes and the better students get at it. Teachers need to provide a safe, nurturing environment, lessons in formats and correct forms, and feedback and response to support student writers' growth.

YESTERDAY'S AND TODAY'S CHALLENGES

Writing, as the second *R* in the traditional reading, writing, and arithmetic curriculum, has been around throughout American education (Coulmas, 1989). Have you ever wondered why, after all this time, there doesn't seem to be complete agreement on how to teach it?

Writing instruction has meant many things to teachers and students over the years. Some have seen it as lessons in spelling, grammar, handwriting, and the simple encoding of words, while others have noted its value in creative expression, as a meaning-making activity, and as an evaluation tool for content areas and literacy assessment. In most cases, it has been viewed as the exclusive responsibility of English language arts teachers throughout elementary and secondary schools.

The issue of correctness in conventional form and visual presentation has shifted from being the most significant aspect of student writing to an important but not always essential feature. Although the relationship between correct conventional features (e.g., grammar, spelling, and handwriting) and written quality (e.g., features centered on ideas, organization, and style) has recurred often throughout the history of U.S. education, it is an issue that is still not completely resolved today. Finding a balance among the important components of well-written compositions is a challenge we invite you to explore with us in this text.

The choice of writing topics is another issue that, while debated thoroughly over the years, is still not firmly resolved. Prominent educators agree that self-selected topics produce improved student writing performance and learning (Atwell, 1998; Calkins, 1994; Graves, 1994; Moffett & Wagner, 1992; Tchudi & Tchudi, 1999). They also suggest that students will write better about those topics with which they already have established background knowledge and understanding. While there is much evidence that writing about familiar, self-selected topics produces more authentic writing and more motivated writers, it does not address the issue of how to assist students with assigned writing assessment topics and written tests in content areas with which they must contend during their educational years. It also does not address teachers' concerns about the availability of writing papers over the Internet, which encourages students to engage in plagiarism. We will look at ways to address both types of writing: divergent, student-centered topics and convergent, instructional-centered assignments.

Finding ways to assess student writing to demonstrate progress and to evaluate for targeting instruction has also been an important issue that continues to demand attention. In content areas, the use of *quick writes* as an exit ticket from a class can provide classroom teachers with important evaluation information about students' perceptions of their subject-matter competencies. Formats like those in the examples at the end of this chapter can help students to practice summarizing, in one or two sentences, the main idea of the lesson or provide lingering questions or concerns they may have on the content. These cards can then be used not only for evaluative purposes and for individual teacher-student dialogue, but they can also serve as a review for the next lesson when they are read aloud to open the next day's lesson.

In terms of evaluating writing proficiency, the two most common ways in which writing assessments are used today are those that measure writing proficiency objectively or holistically and those that use writing to measure content area knowledge. In a later chapter, we will explore some of the issues dealing with writing assessments and how they impact instruction.

Writing, as it connects with speaking, listening, and reading, as well as to other curricular areas, makes it in essence the instructional responsibility of all teachers, not just language arts and/or English teachers. The question of just who is responsible for students' writing throughout their academic classes is another issue that remains unresolved. Writing across the content areas and as an essential part of classroom culture is an important area covered in the next chapter.

LITERACY CONNECTIONS IN YOUR CLASSROOM

Speaking and Writing

Miranda comes into Ms. Fletcher's classroom, chatting happily to her friend Sue. They are going to join the girls in Mrs. Frost's and Mr. Stelling's classes to challenge the boys to a soccer match at lunchtime today. Miranda is animated in her speech. Her hands wave, her head bobs, and her step has a bounce to it that exudes her excited anticipation of showing the boys' team just how skillful the girls have become after numerous practices. Sue doesn't seem to be able to get a word in edgewise.

There isn't enough time to finish their conversation before the bell rings and Ms. Fletcher signals for quiet and the beginning of daily journal writing. Miranda sits silently, staring at the blank journal page, waiting for ideas to happen.

How is it that a chatty student like Miranda, with so much to say, can freeze up in front of a piece of paper? She seems to expect words to appear fully formed from the tip of her pen. She sighs, looks around her, and wonders where the other students seem to be able to find any ideas about which to write.

In the 1960s, Walter Loban (1963) conducted a longitudinal study with over 300 students and found those third graders who wrote well were also above average in speaking and reading. He determined that proficient speaking skills are a necessary prerequisite to learning how to read and write. Somewhat later, a confirming study found a positive relationship between advances in grade and increasing word-length responses (O'Donnell, Griffin, & Norris, 1967).

While the connections are strong, there are some ways to think about how students learn and practice speaking and writing skills to best understand the differences between the two in instruction (see Figure 1.1). While the earliest lessons in speaking typically occur in the limitless hours of a home environment, writing instruction is usually reserved for a specified time frame within formal schooling. Beginning speakers, surrounded by family members who encourage and reward early errors, mispronunciations, and confused meanings with humor and encouragement, are a marked contrast to formal writing instruction, where correctness to form is often stressed from the outset. In comparing early attempts at speech and writing acquisition, this points out the fewer writing possibilities for continued and consistent practice in nonevaluative situations

Figure 1.1   Integration of Speaking and Writing Skills

	Speaking	Writing
When and how learned initially:	Home setting	School setting
Speed of planning and production:	Immediate	Extended over varying time periods
Mode of transmission:	Verbal with nonverbal cues	Manual
Mode of reception:	Listening	Reading
Feedback:	Immediate feedback to clarify and add details	Delayed feedback, recipient must make more inferences
Lexical devices specialized for it:	Somewhat repetitious, self-correcting, slang	More formal and precise
Syntactic devices specialized for it:	Stops and starts Fragments and phrases Lots of pauses, plus "and," "uh," and "um"	Punctuation, capitalization, complete sentences, paragraphing

SOURCE: Adapted from Coulmas, 1989, p. 272.

that are offered to mark an evolving sense of control over conventional forms.

Other notable differences between speaking and writing instruction are the modes of transmission and reception. While writers must rely on more formal and precise devices to communicate their messages, speakers have the additional communicative assistance provided by nonverbal cues as they deliver their message, repeat, and self-correct based on their audience's responses and reactions. As Richard Hughes's (1998) eighth-grade student Angie states,

> There's no worrying about how to say something—I just keep spitting words out until someone interrupts me or I'm understood. Writing is different. I have to be understood without all those things helping me out. Yep, writing has to stand by itself. (p. 89)

However, while speakers have the advantage of nonverbal cues to assist in their message delivery, they also have a limited time to gather their thoughts and deliver a message. Writers, on the other hand, have the security of extended time for written response, thus lessening the possibility of hasty and/or inaccurate responses. This delay provided by the act of writing often gives learners time to revise their messages as they are being delivered.

Connecting oral and written language activities is a circular phenomenon. As children speak about material for a topic on which to write, they are also experimenting with the knowledge they have to construct and write about both real and imaginary experiences. By combining speaking and writing activities, teachers build on the strengths of both spoken and written ways of thinking and communicating and use the social aspects of each to motivate reluctant writers.

Miranda might benefit from interviewing or being interviewed by a classmate about favorites (foods, hobbies, events, pastimes, etc.) and using a tape recorder and graphic organizer to collect the information prior to writing. She could later compare the processes of written and spoken information. (See later chapters for more examples of writing activities involving speaking and writing.) She needs to see the connections between the stories she tells and the stories she can write so she can *talk with a pencil* as well as with her lips.

John, like his classmate James at the opening of this chapter, views writing as a form of punishment, not as a means of making connections between old and new information or even of communicating with others.

Reading and Writing

Ms. Fletcher surveys the class as they are silently reading their social studies books. She notices how unusually attentive John is to the assigned chapter titled "Colonial Society on the Eve of Revolution." As she swings around to the back of the classroom, she notices the small paperback book inserted inside John's textbook. She sighs, walks up behind him, and waits patiently for him to notice her. When he does, she holds out her hand and he deposits the paperback book into it.

"Aw, Ms. Fletcher," he complains as she commandeers the book, "I was just at the good part."

This is not the first time she has had to confiscate a sci-fi or fantasy paperback from John during class time. John is an avid reader and video games player. While Ms. Fletcher is pleased that he is engaged in reading, she is worried that he is too preoccupied with a single genre. She is even more concerned because he refuses to participate in the reading points program at their school. Worst of all, he says he hates to write.

"It kind of ruins the book to have to take a test on it," he explains. "And book reports are dumb. I just want to read the book."

Reading and writing are transactive progressions through which readers and writers negotiate with print to construct meaning on their own. Both processes involve the readers' backgrounds and expectations, the writers' backgrounds and purposes, and the world of the texts themselves. As readers read text, they remember what has been read and also anticipate and predict what the text might say. As writers compose text, they remember what has been said and anticipate what will be said next. Figure 1.2 demonstrates some of the interconnectedness of reading and writing in terms of instruction.

Vocabulary and syntax assist beginning readers and writers in similar ways. Vocabulary studies allow the oral pronunciation and written spelling of words, while instruction in conventional syntax assists in reading and writing words within meaningful contexts. The importance of background knowledge in reading comprehension is well documented (Beck, Perfetti, & McKeown, 1982; Hayes & Tierney, 1982; Rumelhart, 1980); it is equally essential in written composition to write with authority and purpose (Davis & Winek, 1989). Readers need to have a sense of the author's purpose in interpreting constructed meaning, just as writers need to have a sense of audience in constructing interpreted meaning. Sustained practice in both oral and silent reading and writing can lead to improved

Figure 1.2   Interconnections Between Reading and Writing

Reading	Writing
Word study to predict word pronunciation	Word study to predict word spelling
Syntax to process more sophisticated sentences	Syntax to produce more sophisticated sentences
Concept of word to print to read	Concept of word to write
Initial practice by oral rote and repetition	Initial practice by written rote and repetition
Sense of author to help reading comprehension	Sense of audience to help plan, compose, and revise
Prior knowledge is important to comprehend	Prior knowledge is important to write with purpose
Sustained silent reading	Sustained silent writing
Can improve readers' writing development	Can improve writers' reading development
Can provide models for writing	Can create reasons for reading
Learned strategies and practice can improve performance	Learned strategies and practice can improve performance

performance; they are natural partners, as writing can create reasons for reading, while reading can provide models for writing.

Some researchers (Berninger, Abbott, Abbott, Graham, & Richards, 2002) have found that reading comprehension exerts a significant influence on the quality of student writing at Grades 1 through 6. Furthermore, they suggest that it may be the result of an interest in reading literature that inspires a greater interest in composing text and in understanding how authors construct text.

Since the practice of activating prior knowledge (Levin & Pressley, 1981) is important to both reading and writing, it makes sense to use that information in helping both John and James as writers. Since John has so much background knowledge in a single genre, it might make sense to engage him in that genre to work on crafting his writing skills. By building characters, settings, and plots of his own, he can experiment with the form and content of conventional English to provide readers with a story line defined by their shared interests. James, a sports enthusiast, might find satisfaction in recapping a game he has witnessed or in which he has participated.

Writing as a Reward

Writing as a reward, not a punishment, might encourage those students like John and James to change their views on its merits. One of us has successfully used the usually forbidden *note-passing* practice as an incentive for finishing other classroom work. The rules are simple. When your work has been accurately completed and checked by the teacher, you may write notes to anyone in the class. However, they must not contain anything inappropriate or unkind, and they cannot be passed until that person is also finished with his or her work. As an alternative reward, students may also play *dueling pens,* where they draw a controversial topic from a list based on their interests or studies and provided by the teacher (e.g., baseball is the best sport, the movie last night was awful, country music is the best). They silently argue back and forth on paper to present their own side, again mimicking a note-passing situation. (Sometimes they both agree on an issue and they have to flip a coin to see who will present the opposition, or they both can write to both sides, alternating positions.) In any case, writing as an extension of living through a means of communication must be seen as a vital part of their student lives and a reward, not a punishment, in the educational process.

Listening/Viewing and Writing

Ms. Fletcher likes to teach science with lots of hands-on activities, but there are some parts of the science curriculum that she just can't completely cover with hands-on experiments. One of them is black holes, white dwarfs, and neutron stars as wonders of the universe. Therefore, she has obtained a video from the district office that deals with this complex topic. It is brief, only 15 minutes, so she is hoping it will provide enough information to get the class started on this portion of their science unit.

After she briefly introduces the topic and begins to set up the equipment, she acknowledges Tyler's raised hand.

"Can we turn off the lights?" asks Tyler.

"No," replies Ms. Fletcher. "I don't want you zoning out during this film. It's packed with important and interesting information and I want you awake. We'll leave the lights on."

The resulting groans from several of Tyler's friends signaling their disapproval reinforces her conviction that she is correct about the lights-on policy.

During the film, she watches the class, noting their levels of attention, and is gratified at the intensity with which Sam is engaged in the film. His head is forward and his eyes appear transfixed on the screen. She is reassured that, at the end of the film when she reviews the information with questions, Sam at least will have the needed facts and information.

As she flips off the screen, Ms. Fletcher turns to the class and asks, "Who can tell me two interesting facts they just heard in the film?"

No response.

"How about one fact?" she tries.

Tyler's hand comes up. "The part about black holes not radiating light, and that if an object falls inside a black hole, it doesn't emit light either. That's why finding black holes is so hard."

"Great," replies Ms. Fletcher as she writes this on the board for all to see. She is somewhat surprised at his answer, since he appeared to be doodling on a piece of scratch paper during the entire film. Since she is writing, she calls on Sam to add more information. He can be talking while she finishes writing Tyler's ideas on the board.

"Sam, how about you? What was something you found interesting?"

"I don't know," said Sam. "I wasn't really listening."

Ms. Fletcher turns and, seeing Diane's hand up, calls on her next. However, she is wondering how Sam could not be listening, when he seemed so intent.

Active listening and/or viewing—that is, participating in an event beyond the semiconscious world of the mandated lecture or video series— provide students with models for thinking about and conversing about topics and processes. By actively questioning and engaging in new information, students can be led to question ideas, present solutions to problems, and collect information on which to write. Imitation is a natural means by which people have learned for centuries. Viewing and listening provide the example for such imitation.

While we often consider having students produce a piece of writing after a film or other type of presentation, using writing before a viewing event can be even more important. Sam might have been a more efficient listener if he had engaged in some writing prior to watching the film. Discussion following the viewing could also begin with individual writing to allow for personal differences and unique thought processes prior to the discussion, which can sometimes lead students on paths other than their own.

Listening is also an important aspect of the writing process, certainly in terms of peer response. Donald Graves (2004) suggests that children need to earn the right to ask questions or make suggestions by first showing they are good listeners. One technique suggested by Graves is requiring those who wish to make comments or ask questions to first engage in dialogue with the author and audience by summarizing a piece of writing, restating important details, or suggesting the focus of the piece of writing. This practice assists both the writer and the listeners in developing important literacy skills and in remaining actively engaged in the process. It provides the listener with practice in summarizing strategies and with an awareness of the author's efforts. In addition, it is a means of helping the writer to discover how the message is being perceived.

Questions to or responses from students:

1. Restate as many details as you can from the piece.

2. What is the main focus of the piece?

3. What do you think the author wants you as the reader to know, think, feel?

4. What is the most vivid impression you have from the piece?

5. What do you want to know more about?

Another means of assisting with the listening-writing connection is to provide opportunities for *second-chance listening*. After providing students with a purpose for listening and/or viewing and participating in the production, have them write out all they can remember. Then replay the audio or video and have them add details and sequencing to revise their original writing. An alternate type of activity might be to have students, after the first viewing or at a re-viewing, write out questions, then sort questions by category. Topics for reports can be brainstormed from question categories.

THE THREE HARDEST CHALLENGES IN HELPING STUDENT WRITERS

Getting Them Started

Perhaps the most difficult part of helping students to write is to get them started. That blank page is daunting, even for adults. As mentioned previously, the single best way to get your students engaged so they can learn and practice the craft of writing is to help them in self-selecting topics of interest on which to write. The support of writing about a subject of interest can help provide sufficient motivation to work on the processes of idea gathering, organizing, word crafting, experimenting with style, and editing for conventions. However, you need to know your students well to help guide them in this process.

Interest inventories that focus on your students' current literacy lives can provide a good starting place, especially at the beginning of the year. See the end of this chapter for student interest inventories for primary (K–1), intermediate (2–4), and middle (5–8) grades. These provide a good starting place for teachers to plan instruction in a way that meets their students' individual needs and interests.

Individual or small group conferences with students can also help teachers in finding possible topics of interest and assisting students with connecting their topics and collaborating with one another. For example, if two students are studying adjoining states that share a natural landform like mountains or a river, they can collaborate on sources and even compare how that landform influences each area in similar or different ways. Or, as another example, if several students are studying various animals, they can collaborate on some generalizations that can be made about these animals as vertebrates or invertebrates.

While self-selected topics have become the accepted custom because of their motivating aspect for real writing, students throughout their educational lives do not always have the luxury of selecting their own topics. They need strategies for dealing with the assigned topic as well. Self-questioning strategies to help collect information, graphic organizers to arrange information, and revision strategies to ensure complete responses are covered in Chapter 5.

Keeping Them Going

Student understanding and practice in a writing process follows a scaffolding sequence from teacher-directed to more student-centered, independent writing. It begins with teacher-*modeled* writing, where the teacher writes to a topic while *thinking aloud* and demonstrates decisions made as a piece of writing progresses. It advances to *shared* writing, where the teacher and students think together and the teacher writes a collaborative piece with ideas and information collected from the class and the teacher. In *interactive* writing, the next step in the progression toward independent writing, the teacher and students also collaborate with the writing; however, the students *share the pen* with the teacher and one another. They take turns writing the ideas in a list or cluster, adding words and sentences, making corrections, and discussing choices in the writing. In *guided* writing, the teacher sets up the writing activity through a focused lesson, and students write, sometimes independently and sometimes in groups, with teacher supervision and guidance. *Independent* writers apply and practice all the skills and strategies learned using self-selected topics, and the teacher acts as a monitor and coach to support them in writing workshop-type activities.

Getting Them Finished

Helping students to become task oriented and to meet deadlines is an important life skill that many procrastinating adults have yet to master. Monitoring student activity to help them to use their time wisely, breaking down large tasks into smaller, more manageable ones, and helping set short-term goals are important parts of the writing process that require much teacher attention.

Students need assistance in setting and meeting realistic targets for working on their writing. Sometimes this needs to begin as very small baby steps. "In the next five minutes, write one or two sentences about your topic" or "Write a who, what, where, when, why, or how question about your piece of writing and then answer it in a complete sentence. See if you can add that to your piece of writing so far."

Techniques for student conferences and checklists for revision will be covered in Chapter 4. However, one of the most valuable tools available for student learners is to assist them in short- and long-term goal setting within a responsibility framework that can be consistently monitored for progress.

Getting them to *the end* of collecting and writing down ideas is not the completion of work on a piece of writing. There is still the matter of correct standard usage and forms, maybe the most difficult of all in the process for student writers. How can teachers get students to really revise and not simply supply surface edits? Which conventions are most important for mastery at which points in a student writer's school history? How can teachers make sure students review and edit all the possible errors in their writing? How much correcting is *too much* correcting?

The issue of correctness to form and conventions, even with the assistance of word processing software with spelling and grammar checks, is still an issue today. The balance between providing instruction and emphasis on form and conventions over attention to ideas and content is a difficult decision for most teachers, especially as they try to engage and motivate student writers to experiment with longer and more complex writing styles.

WRITING TOGETHER AS A WAY OF COMMUNICATING, LEARNING, AND MEANING-MAKING

Miss Eastman, a university preservice student visiting Ms. Fletcher's class, flips open her cell phone, lights flash, and she starts punching buttons rapidly.

"Are you calling someone?" asks Marissa, as she lines up with the rest of the class for lunch and recess.

Several other students move out of line and crowd around Miss Eastman, curious about her communication with her "outside" life.

"No, I'm just sending an instant message to my brother. I forgot to feed the cat, and she'll probably register her anger by shredding the dining room curtains. I'm telling him to get cat food on his way home from school."

"How do you know which buttons to push?" asks James, leaning over to place his head directly in front of Miss Eastman's line of vision with the receiver.

"Well, see how each button has letters on it as well as numbers? I use the letters on the keypad to spell out my message, like this."

She demonstrates the process for them.

The class is fascinated with the speed with which the message is relayed as well as the lights and sounds of the phone.

The use of writing and reading as a fast, efficient means of communicating has advanced with new technologies and made writing an essential skill in navigating new systems of information. E-mail communications, instant messaging, and chat rooms have launched writing as a communications tool into an important realm that requires succinct and fluent writing skills.

In fact, the text messaging that was a novelty to these younger students has quickly evolved to become a banned digital note-sending device in some school settings and is beginning to evolve again as cell phones morph into the next classroom-incorporated digital learning device.

In addition, writing can help students to see the implications of the things they are learning throughout the curriculum. In reading and writing about texts, they appreciate the details and explanations that parts make of a whole, an important aspect of problem solving. By working from different perspectives and in different contexts in a community of writers, students learn to appreciate complexity and controversy as well as the viewpoints of others. Revision as a result of peer response or self-editing moves students to problem-finding situations. Exploring new questions and multifaceted challenges in all content areas promotes a deeper understanding of improving their environment and taking a critical stance to become informed citizens.

"So, Julio," the visiting Miss Eastman remarks, trying in her most sociable soon-to-be-teacher manner to engage this brand new student in talk about his writing. His name tag, prominently displayed on his desk, is brightly colored with zigzags and stars, a sure sign of creative talent. *"Can you tell me a bit about what you are writing?"*

He looks up at her blankly. She sees he has only managed to write two sentences on his paper, and the class began writing about 30 minutes ago. That's quite a bit of writing time without much to show for his efforts. She wonders, *Do you suppose those sentences are just copied from one of the motivational posters from around the room?* She tries again.

"Will you read me your story? So I can hear your words?" she cajoles, hoping at least for a yes or no response. Again, those bright eyes return a vacant stare.

"Miss Eastman?" Marissa hails her from the set of desks two rows back. *"Miss Eastman, Julio doesn't speak any English. He doesn't understand you."*

Forehead slapping time. Looking more closely, she sees that Julio's sentences are written in Spanish. What was she thinking?! And now what is she supposed to do? She hasn't encountered this in the texts she has read about engaging students with writing. The authors talk about having rich discussions and having students write and talk and respond in oral discourse. She asks Marissa, who knows some of both languages, to join them.

"Can you help me to understand what Julio is saying on his paper?" she asks. Marissa looks at the paper and speaks quickly in Spanish to Julio and he responds in kind.

"He is writing that he is hungry and can't wait for lunch."

"I'm hungry too," she replies. She leans over on his paper and writes, *"Julio is hungry. I am hungry too."* With a combination of gestures and pointing to the words, she reads it aloud to Julio. He smiles.

With the help of Ms. Fletcher and her students, Miss Eastman has grown in her appreciation of the diversity of learners' needs, and the entire class will together come to new ways of knowing and understanding through writing.

Exit Cards

These can be on index cards for individual students in a class. For teachers with multiple classes, you can cut up construction paper so there is one color for each of your classes, and during the last 5–10 minutes of class, one or two times a week, students can spend the last several minutes writing to you about what they've learned or failed to learn and what you might be able to do to help.

10-Minute Quick-write

Here's what I've learned this week.

10-Minute Write-in Requests

What do you want to learn more about tomorrow?

10-Minute Survey

I'm sponsoring a survey.

What was something new you learned today?

What was the best part about this week's class?

10-Minute RFA (Request for Assistance)

Here's what I need more help with in today's class.

Some things you could do to help me might be . . .

10 Minute Survey

What was the best part about this week's class?

10-Minute Write-in Requests

Write about an important "aha!" you may have had during class today.

10 Minute Evaluation

Write an evaluation of your performance in class today.

What did you do well? On what other things do you want to work?

10 Minute Quick Check

Write 3 test items you can answer that demonstrate what you learned today.

INVENTORY 1.1

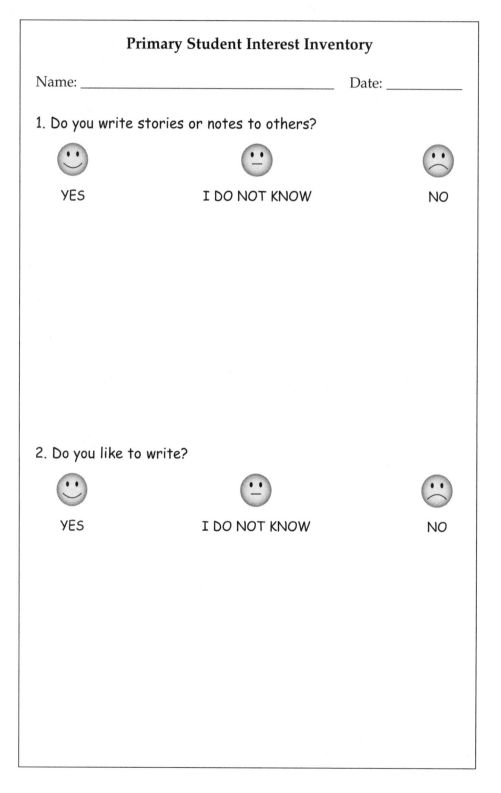

Primary Student Interest Inventory

Name: _____ Date: _____

1. Do you write stories or notes to others?

YES   I DO NOT KNOW   NO

2. Do you like to write?

YES   I DO NOT KNOW   NO

3. Show me what you like to write about.

4. Do you want to learn how to write things to other people?

YES   I DO NOT KNOW   NO

INVENTORY 1.2

Primary Student Interest Inventory (Grades 2-3)

Name: _____ Date: _____

1. Do you like to write?   YES   NO

2. Do you sometimes write at home?   YES   NO

3. Do you need a starter?   Never   Sometimes   Always

4. To whom do you like to write?

5. How do you get your ideas for writing?

6. What is easy and what is hard about writing?

7. Do you like to share your writing?

8. Do you want to learn more about writing?

INVENTORY 1.3

Transitioning Student Interest Inventory (Grades 3-4)

Name: _____ Date: _____

1. Do you consider yourself a writer?   YES   NO

2. Why do we write? What are some good reasons?

3. What do you like to write?

4. What does someone have to know to write well?

5. How often do you write at home?

6. How do you feel about using free time during the school day for writing?

INVENTORY 1.4

Intermediate Student Interest Inventory

Name: _____   Date: _____

1. Do you like to write?   YES   NO

2. Do you sometimes write at home?   YES   NO

3. Do you need a starter?   Never   Sometimes   Always

4. To whom do you like to write?

5. How do you get your ideas for writing?

6. What is easy and what is hard about writing?

7. Do you like to share your writing?

8. Do you want to learn more about writing?

INVENTORY 1.5

Middle Grades Student Interest Inventory

Name: _____ Date: _____

1. What is the easiest part of writing for you? The most difficult?

2. How do you start a piece of writing? How do you find out what you want to say?

3. How do you know when a piece of writing is finished? How do you decide you are "done"?

4. What do you think are the characteristics of "good writing"? Is most of your writing good writing? Why or why not?

5. What instructions have you been given in writing stories and/or informational text? Do you follow them? If no one has ever taught you how to write, how did you learn?

6. If given the choice of free time in school, how often might you choose to write?

INVENTORY 1.6

Middle Grades Student Interest Inventory (Grades 7-8)

Name: _____ Date: _____

Rank: 5 – strongly agree
       4 – agree
       3 – disagree
       2 – strongly disagree
       1 – no opinion

1. I like to write.   5   4   3   2   1

2. I worry about getting poor
    grades when I do writing assignments.   5   4   3   2   1

3. I am able to write on many different
    subjects and for different people.   5   4   3   2   1

4. I worry a great deal about spelling
    and grammar when I write.   5   4   3   2   1

5. I enjoy sharing my writing with others.   5   4   3   2   1

6. I would rather pick my own topic than
    be provided with a prompt when I write.   5   4   3   2   1

7. I like to use the computer instead
    of paper and pencil/pen when I have
    to do some of my own writing.   5   4   3   2   1

8. Describe some occasions where you seem to do your best writing.

9. What are some things your teacher can do to help you succeed as a
   writer?

2 Writing About Information

Jaryd looks through his book about George Washington. He smiles to a friend and shows him a picture of Washington that he has found. "I think this will work for the cover of my report." He proceeds to draw a version of this illustration on the cover of his report about Washington. Eric, who sits near him, is working on a patriot report as well. "I need more information about John Hancock." He decides to use the Internet to find more information. Jaryd goes with Eric to the classroom computer to see what he can find as well. Both boys leave the computer chatting about the handfuls of printouts with information about their patriot. They sift through the information and add important details to their individual reports. Jaryd chats with Eric about each new discovery he makes about Washington and his life. Eric provides Jaryd with information about John Hancock and George Washington, which Jaryd places into his report.

In the past, scenes like the one above were typical in middle school and high school classrooms. However, today this type of research quest and writing is seen in elementary school classrooms like the one that Jaryd and Eric are a part of. In the above scenario, the boys were working on a report that connected to their social studies curriculum. Their third-grade teacher decided to extend her curriculum and her students' understanding of early U.S. patriots by having each student complete an extended report. To accomplish this task, she provided numerous reference books, the class text, and Internet resources for her students' research. In addition, she developed a research format for students where they wrote discrete sections for each major area related to their patriot. For example, there were sections on the patriot's early life, important accomplishments, and so on. Through scaffolding a report in this way, these young students were successful in producing a longer piece of writing that was revised, edited, and polished for classroom sharing.

This chapter centers on informal and formal writing about content, with the primary purpose of deepening student understanding. The chapter begins with informal writing, most often first draft writing, where students quickly share current understandings. From these more informal jottings, the chapter moves to considering more formal writing about content, as was shared in the above scenario. The chapter ends with a description of the connections between reading and writing informational text and how students can be supported as they come to understand their structures.

INFORMAL WRITING

In 1970, Britton wrote about expressive writing, the informal language that we use every day to communicate. He saw expressive language as an important tool for learning, as this language allows students to explore and assimilate new ideas and experiences. Armbruster (2000) describes this writing as writing to learn. After reviewing the research centered on writing to learn, she concluded that writing assists learning of content knowledge.

In this section, we explore low-stakes writing, or informal writing to learn. Many times it serves as informal, ongoing assessment of students' current knowledge about a topic. This writing is first draft writing, meant only for the students' own use, that often has errors in spelling and punctuation. The goal of this writing is for students to express their feelings and thoughts about ideas. Although teachers are concerned about writing conventions and their development, they know that this writing is meant for clarification and the extension of ideas. Vacca and Vacca (2000) observed that students think and write more when engaged in low-stakes writing, where the focus is only on idea sharing.

Following are several examples of informal writing to learn. They represent the work of students from many grade levels who are exploring a variety of content areas. While the examples are rich and varied, they do not cover all of the content disciplines. Because not all disciplines are represented, it does not mean that writing is not appropriate as a tool to expand and clarify thinking in these areas. So, for example, teachers of art, health, and physical education would also have numerous opportunities where informal writing is appropriate.

What is similar in all of the examples is that teachers gave students time to reflect on their learning through writing. Following writing, they either engaged students in conversation or they wrote comments to students about their ideas. The goals of informal writing are the following:

1. Student's clarification and extension of thinking about a content area or topic.

2. Student's and teacher's understanding of misconceptions or incomplete knowledge of the content area or topic to serve as a basis for further instruction.

Writing About Mathematics

We have two examples to share centered on mathematics. One is grounded in direct classroom instruction and the other is focused on independent work completed by a student as homework.

The first example occurred during a mathematics lesson in a sixth-grade classroom. Following is the conversation that Ms. Moore shared with her students:

Ms. Moore: Please take out your notebooks. We are going to create notes on how to solve mathematic word problems. What is the first thing we do to solve a problem?

Child: We read it and try to understand it.

Ms. Moore: That is right. You need to understand what you are looking for, what they are asking. Remember yesterday when we had to know how many chickens and how many cows the farmer had?

Child: Then we made a plan. I drew the problem.

Ms. Moore: Yes, and it worked. Sometimes drawing won't work. So how about if we make a list on how to solve a problem.

Child: Draw a picture.

Child: Use numbers.

Child: Make a table.

Child: Act it out.

Ms. Moore: So let's write these ideas in our notebook. Then when you solve a problem, I want you to write how you solved the problem and your opinion of how your strategy worked.

Today our problem is this. You have 13 students in the room. We have 38 books that need to be distributed. Each student is to get two books. There are 14 copies of one book and 24 copies of another book. Are there enough books? Are there any left over? How did you solve your problem? What do you think about this solution?

The students solved this problem individually. After they finished, they shared their solutions with students at their table. Then the teacher created a graph showing how the students in the class solved this problem. Figures 2.1 and 2.2 are two examples of their solutions.

Figure 2.1 Maria's Solution

I need to know if books are left over.

13 students

14 book 1

38 book 2

Book 1 – one for each and 1 left over—I just subtracted 14 – 13 = 1

Book 2 – I divided 38 by 2 so there were two groups of 19. Then I passed out one book to each student. I had 6 books left in Group 1. I had 19 books left in Group 2. I added 19 + 6 and I know there were 25 too many.

There were enough books and I had 26 extra books.

I liked the way I solved the Book 1 problem. I think there is an easier way to solve Book 2. Maybe I could have just subtracted and not divided.

Figure 2.2 Anna's Solution

Okay I need to pass out books. There are 13 kids. So the first book is easy; there is 1 left. I just know that. The second book is trickier because there are 38 and there are 13 kids. I drew a line for each student, and I counted a book for each of them. So I needed 13. Then I subtracted 13 from 38 to get my answer of 25.

I, I, I, I, I, I, I, I, I, I, I

I wanted to draw a book, but I ran out of time. I ran out of time when I started to draw.

In these examples, both students arrived at the correct answer. Because the students were able to solve this problem, Ms. Moore decided that she would move to problems with more than one operation. She also needed to work with Maria to make sure that she used the most efficient process when solving verbal problems and with Anna so that she could move beyond drawing when drawing was unnecessary. Ms. Moore was pleased with this early writing about mathematics because she had a better idea of the processes her students used when solving word problems, not just whether they arrived at the correct answer.

In the second example, Ms. Schneider, a fifth-grade teacher, assigned mathematics homework to her students. She asked her students to consider their mathematics charts (e.g., multiplication and division) and then answer specific questions such as what multiples are highlighted and which multiples are even or odd numbers. In Figure 2.3 an example of one student's response is shared.

The value of this more extended mathematics assignment is the focus on the child's thinking as he or she engages in a mathematical exploration. As seen in LaQuisha's example, students can engage in this process independently. Most important, the teacher can use this writing as a window into a child's understanding, and thus it serves as informal assessment as well.

Figure 2.3   LaQuisha's Homework

> When I looked at multiples of 12, I saw 3, 4, 6, and 2. Three was odd and the others are even numbers. All the charts had the 2 highlighted, but none had the 3, 4, or 6 highlighted. None of the multiples had only odd numbers. I don't know why. It was easy to find the multiples with 2. Then I looked at numbers that are multiplied by 12, like 72 and 84. I never thought about these before. I think this is easy when I have the charts. The 12s are hard to remember without the charts.

Writing About Science

We have included three examples where students have written about science content they are studying. The first example is from a kindergarten student, the second from a first-grade student, and the third from a sixth-grade student. Most important, these examples demonstrate that students as young as five years of age can write and/or draw about informational content, although it can be more difficult to read.

In Figure 2.4, Noah wrote about spiders. His kindergarten teacher organized a unit of study centered on spiders. Each day, the students

Figure 2.4 Noah's Writing About Spiders

wrote one fact that they knew about spiders. At the end of the unit, each child's facts were compiled into a book that they shared with the class and their parents. Noah's example shows his focus on the number of legs that a spider has. While there are spelling and punctuation errors, his writing content shows that he is accurate about this one fact about spiders.

Kennady's teacher also organized her science instruction around units of study. Toward the end of the first-grade year, she taught her students about the rain forest. At the conclusion of the unit, she was curious about what her students remembered best. She asked each student to write about the rain forest. She provided no further directions, as she wanted to discover their individual understandings. Kennady's writing is shared in Figure 2.5. She has identified several major facts about the rain forest. These include a focus on its layers and the birds and their attributes. What is particularly interesting in this example is her ability to share ideas and include punctuation and the correct spelling of the majority of words simultaneously.

The last example comes from a science notebook that a sixth-grade student kept as he studied sound waves. Each day he wrote a fact, similar to what happened in the kindergarten example (see Figure 2.6). He also recorded his thoughts after science experiments.

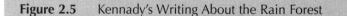

Figure 2.5   Kennady's Writing About the Rain Forest

> The rain forest has four layers in it. they are emergent, canopy, understory, and forest floor. Rainforest birds stand on one foot and eat with the other. Rainforest birds acsoly camoflosh into green trees some animels think they are frots or flawers.

As with the mathematics examples, these show the thinking of students as they come to understand science content. In the last example, the teacher learns that this student has defined major ideas when studying sound waves. However, when the student described his experiment, he

Figure 2.6   Sound Wave Notebook Entries

1. A sound wave is a vibration moving through matter.

2. A vibration is a back-and-forth movement.

3. Frequency is how fast something is vibrating.

Experiment – I felt a loud explosion. It felt like someone was punching my face. I heard it like a guy shooting. The vibration went back and forth when I yelled into the machine. [Spelling and punctuation corrected.]

failed to include this vocabulary in any meaningful way; rather, he focused on personal connections. This knowledge suggests that the teacher participate in a conversation with this student where he utilizes the important vocabulary to determine if he truly understands what the terms mean and how they were demonstrated in the experiment.

Writing About Social Studies

The student example of writing about social studies comes from Lucero, a sixth-grade student. Lucero's classroom consisted predominantly of students who learned English when they arrived at the school door. Her teacher, Mrs. Hunter, consistently had her students write about social studies content because she wanted them to move beyond surface understanding. For each unit of study, students kept notebooks where they added new information each day. The routine was that social studies instruction began with students' sharing interesting information that they discovered. The teacher then directed a lesson that extended their knowledge. At the conclusion of the lesson, students had 10 minutes to add to their notes. After writing, they shared one bit of information with the students at their table. By their reading, writing, and talking about Greece, Mrs. Hunter knew that her students understood her instruction and were familiar with this ancient civilization.

In Figure 2.7 there are snippets from the notes that Lucero kept when they studied ancient Greece. Lucero's notebook continued for several pages. Her teacher had students organize their ideas by topic, as seen in Lucero's writing about family life and food. At the end of the Greece study, the students created individual reports about one element of life in ancient Greece. They used their daily jottings and thoughts as the core of this report.

Mrs. Hunter said, "It takes longer to cover material when students write and talk, but they remember and understand more." She found that

Figure 2.7	Lucero's Notebook About Greece

Family Life – Men ran the government, and spent a great deal of their time away from home. When they were home, they oversaw slaves working on crops, sailing, hunting, or trading.

Greek women had almost no freedom. They could go to weddings and funerals. They could visit their neighbors. They had to run the house and have children. They were lucky that they didn't have to clean the house, because they had slaves.

Food – They had a lot to eat. They grew olives, grapes, and figs. They had goats for milk and cheese. They grew wheat for bread. They caught fish and they made wine.

having her students who were new to English write and discuss strengthened their understandings, especially in subject areas like social studies that were abstract in content and heavily loaded with vocabulary not familiar to them.

Writing About Vocabulary

Most teachers are familiar with the practice of having students look up words in a dictionary, write their definitions, and then use them in a sentence. While this practice does not really help students remember word meanings, it is one that is still commonly used (Bear, Invernizzi, Templeton, & Johnston, 2000).

The example in Figure 2.8 displays another way for students to come to know and remember new vocabulary words. Writing about words can cross all subject matter areas.

Cory's exploration demonstrates his focus on the meaning of the root *sub*. As he collects words with *sub* in them, he continues to explore meaning, rather than just spelling or remembering a simple definition. Word explorations like this allow students to generate the meanings and spellings of new words that are connected by a common root.

FORMAL WRITING

In contrast to informal writing to learn, formal writing carries more expectations. In formal writing, students are still concerned with clarity and accuracy of the information they share, but they also need to revise and edit their writing before sharing it. Often the format for this writing is a

Figure 2.8   Cory's Exploration of the Root *Sub*

Subject – Dictionary – something thought or talked about or a course or field that is studied

Substance – a material

Subconscious – the part of the mind where dreaming happens

I still don't know what sub means. I am thinking a part of something.

Subtract – take away from

Submerge – to cover with water

Subway – an underground train

Maybe sub means under and a part of something. I need to find more sub words to know for sure.

report, similar to the one described in the introductory vignette. This type of writing is also often used in assessments. See Chapter 5 for more information on writing assessments.

For informal writing, students typically respond to one problem, experiment, or book, often the textbook. In formal writing, students consolidate information across texts, known as discourse synthesis (Spivey, 1990). A discourse synthesis requires that students select, organize, and connect information from several sources. The decisions that students make in determining the credibility of sources and which information to include are complex. Teachers certainly play a critical part in helping students contemplate criteria for these decisions.

Report Writing

We share several examples of the strategies used and sections of reports completed by elementary students. The examples come from second- to sixth-grade students. In Figure 2.9, Jaryd's final report on George Washington is shared. Jaryd chose a birth-to-death organization. He starts with interesting details about Washington's family. The middle of his report shares details about Washington's life. He concludes with a paragraph about his death. This organization parallels the note-taking strategies required by his teacher.

After Jaryd shared his report, his teacher asked him how he found all of his information. He answered, "I read three chapter books and I found information on the Internet. I had to read a book that was above my level.

Figure 2.9 Jaryd's George Washington Report

George Washington

George Washington was born in Virginia on a farm on February 22, 1732. He was the oldest son. He had two half brothers.

When George was eleven, his father died. George's half brother Lawrence raised him. George married Martha Custis in 1759. They lived at Mount Vernon. Their house was built from wood.

George Washington was a leader of the French and Indian War and the Patriot War. In one battle, George's coat was shot through with bullet holes, but he was okay. John Hancock was jealous of George Washington for being a leader of the army. Washington was even the leader at the Constitutional Convention. Many wanted him to be the president. On April 30, 1789 he became the first American president.

Two years after he quit being the president, George caught a cold while riding a horse in a rainstorm. On December 17, 1799 he died. He was buried at Mount Vernon. [no spelling or punctuation changes from original]

It took me a week but I found out when he was born and when he died. Eric told me about John Hancock because that was the patriot he was studying." This information, along with the written report, allowed the teacher to discover Jaryd's content knowledge about George Washington and the process he used to discover this information. His teacher knew that

1. Jaryd can find information from multiple sources and synthesize it for a report.

2. He knows how to use books and the Internet to find information.

3. He can share this information in a report that is cohesive.

4. He can revise and edit his work for public sharing.

Josie was also expected to write a report at the conclusion of her sixth-grade exploration of the Mayan and Anasazi cultures. Her teacher left the format of the report up to individual students. In addition to learning about these cultures, Josie completed a prewriting organizational scheme to guide her writing. Her prewriting planning is shared in Figure 2.10. From this planning, she wrote an essay that focused on the disappearance of these cultures (see Figure 2.11).

Figure 2.10 Josie's Prewriting

Beginning – How did the Anasazi and Mayans disappear? The world doesn't know. I will gather facts and build my own theory.

Middle – The Mayans and Anasazi were farmers and they were famous. Details and facts.

End – End of facts. Another culture invaded them and no one knew about the war. A disease spread and killed them. They were poisoned.

Figure 2.11 Josie's Disappearance Report

Disappearance

Why did the Mayans and Anasazi disappear? I have a theory. First, let's look at the facts! The Mayans had a religious culture. The early Mayans were delighted by the achievements of the Olmec people, and they admired the Teothucans' civilization. The Mayans liked other cultures, like the Mesoamericans, because they were religious.

Now they sound like a really religious culture, but why would they disappear? So let's check and see if other cultures disappeared. The Anasazi were a Northern American people. They were never Mexican or other cultures. They were great farmers and they planted corn, cabbage, beans, and carrots. The Anasazi adapted to their harsh desert environment. They even went on a diet when they hunted deer, rabbits, and bighorn sheep.

Wow, that is a lot of information. But my theory is that the Mayans left because they were inspired by the Teothucans' civilization. So they had a secret war that killed all of them and left no evidence. The second theory is for the Anasazi people. Since they were good planters and used the food they planted, they didn't notice the drug that grew in the food. When they ate it, they all died together. These people were religious so this may have been part of a ceremony.

As you can tell, I am trying to create theories of why these people disappeared. Do come with me and we can seek the truth together.

Josie's essay is very different from most. She has engaged her audience through questions and her quest for answers. She has used some facts to build theories about the disappearance of ancient peoples. Certainly, she could have added more details, but what is particularly interesting is the way she has used her knowledge and experiences to shape reasons for the disappearance of these cultures. Her voice is also very strong in this writing as she convinces her audience that her theories have foundation and are possible solutions.

The final example comes from a second-grade classroom where students completed a report on an animal. Unlike Josie's teacher, the teacher of these young students provided a very structured format for the report. Students were expected to name and describe their animal; provide the characteristics, defenses, food, habitat, and predators of the animal; discuss protections, if any, for the animal; and provide a reference section. Students did not have the Internet for research, but they did have numerous magazines and books.

Ben decided to study the poison dart frog for his animal. Each section of his report was a page with an illustration. In Figure 2.12, one page of his report is shared. Ben, like Josie and Jaryd, used multiple sources to get information for his report. Unlike the other two, he did not synthesize this information; rather, he used one source for each part of his report. This strategy is common for students when they begin to use multiple sources for report writing.

In these examples, the variation of support and expectations are noted. For younger students, teachers tend to structure the expectations of the report more clearly. They also have students construct their notes around discrete topics that can then be combined into a full report. For older students, as seen in Josie's report, there is more freedom in structure and prewriting activities. A commonality across this more formal writing is that students revise and edit and present a cohesive report that is free of punctuation and spelling errors to others.

Concept-Oriented Reading Instruction (CORI)

In the report writing section, it was clear that teachers created the structures for student reports. Guthrie and his colleagues (1996) decided to study a program they developed that facilitated student learning of informational text through reading and writing. Their program has four phases:

1. Observe and personalize. Students observe their environment and decide what they might want to study.

2. Search and retrieve. Students are taught to use the library, to find informational science texts, and to search these books to find answers to their questions.

3. Comprehend and integrate. Students read, summarize, take notes, and reflect critically on their information.

4. Communicate to others. Students present their discoveries to others through journal entries, reports, class books, or informational stories.

Figure 2.12 Ben's Poison Dart Report

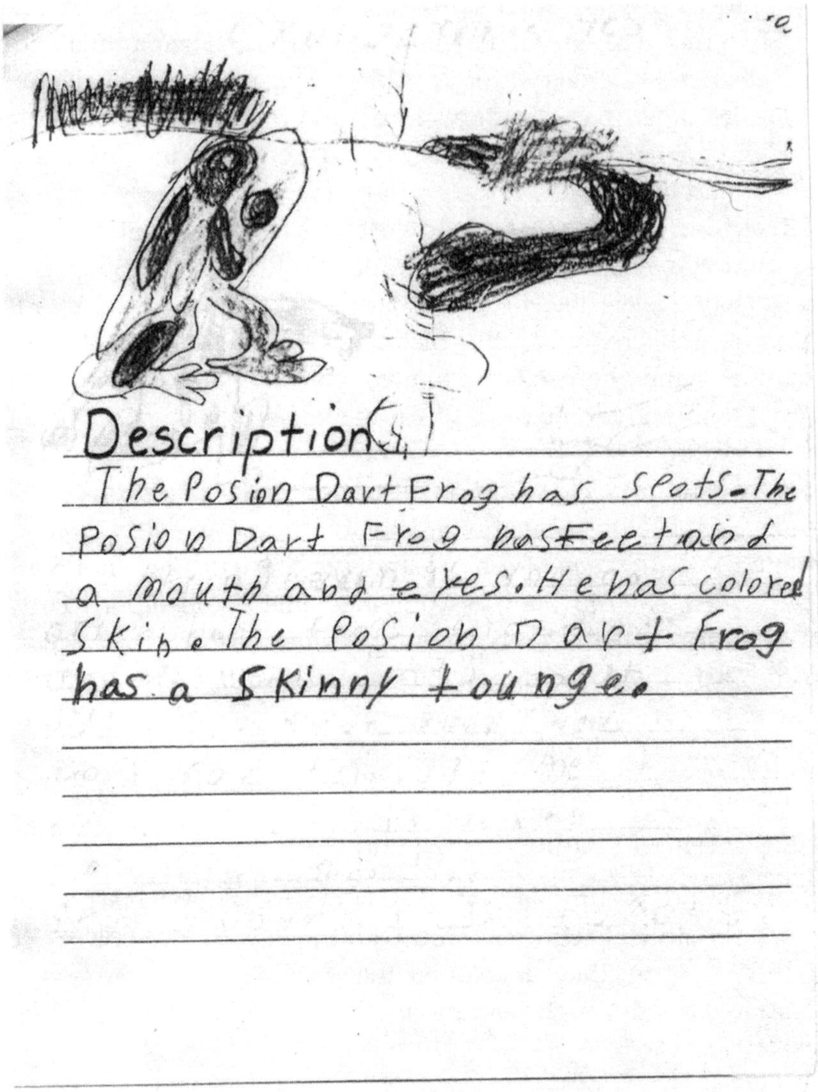

Description.

The Posion Dart Frog has spots. The Posion Dart Frog has Feet and a mouth and eyes. He has colored Skin. The Posion Dart Frog has a skinny tounge.

CORI has been studied in third- and fifth-grade classrooms. The results of these investigations indicate that students made gains in their ability to search multiple texts, represent knowledge, transfer concepts, comprehend informational text, and interpret text. In addition, students demonstrated greater conceptual learning and high engagement with CORI activities.

Teachers have used this program to organize content studies. For example, they select a required topic from their curriculum. From this topic, they have students generate questions that are personally meaningful to them. Once questions are developed, the teacher and students find pertinent reference material. Then students engage in reading, summarizing, drawing, and any other note-taking formats. Once suitable answers are discovered, each student conferences with his or her teacher to decide how this information will be shared. CORI is a structured format that assists teachers and students with content explorations. It is similar to report writing in that all of the notes are synthesized for a report that must meet the demands of an audience.

CONNECTIONS BETWEEN INFORMATIONAL TEXT AND STUDENT WRITING

As students read and write about information, they learn that informational texts are organized very differently than narrative texts (Casbergue & Plauche, 2003). For instance, there is no plot and characters are not evident. These texts also serve as a model for the informational writing that students will be doing as they explore topics in depth. Because children as young as those in preschool can engage with informational text (Duke, Bennett-Armistead, & Roberts, 2003), teachers are facilitating the reading and writing of these texts in preschool and elementary grades.

Organizations of Informational Text

Description

Authors use description to describe a topic and to provide examples of it. Jaryd learned about this kind of informational writing when he researched George Washington. Other examples are prevalent in describing animals, plants, people, events, and so on.

Teachers often help students with descriptive writing by identifying a topic for writing and meaningful categories surrounding it. As a prewriting activity, students often brainstorm around the categories. For example, if students were studying fruit, each student might pick a fruit to write about. For a child who picked apples, he or she might have categories such as kinds of apples, parts of apples, how and where apples grow, and so on. These categories then provide the structure for the written report.

Sequence

This structure is similar to the narrative: What happened first, then, and finally? However, the sequence organization of writing in informational text is not a plot. Rather, this type of structure explains an order of steps or a process. For example, this format is often used in biographies and in science to share the evolution of a caterpillar to a butterfly, for instance.

Teachers often help students write in this structure by giving them a numbered paper or a chart that lists first, then, then, and last. Students fill these in as they describe a process or the important events in the life of a person they are studying. Jaryd's writing about George Washington followed this structure in which he began with his early life, then his career, and last his death.

Cause-Effect

This sequence involves describing causes that lead to a result. They could be the causes that led to a war. They could be the description of a science experiment and then the result.

Teachers can support students with this structure by supplying a diagram similar to the one shown in Figure 2.13. Here students were exploring how we came to have an American flag. They started with the effect of a national flag. Then they generated possible causes that they were going to explore.

Problem-Solution

This structure is similar to cause and effect. Students must understand a problem well enough to offer solutions. Josie demonstrated her attempt at a problem-solution piece of informational writing when she attempted to explain why the Anasazi and Mayans disappeared.

Not surprising is that a graphic support for problem-solution writing is similar to the one described for cause-effect. Students can begin with the problem and then identify potential solutions.

Compare-Contrast

This format provides for comparison of two events, people, animals, or objects, for example. This is a more difficult structure than the others described, as students are now expected to move beyond a single focus for writing to compare and contrast two people, events, and so on. This requires extensive knowledge of both topics.

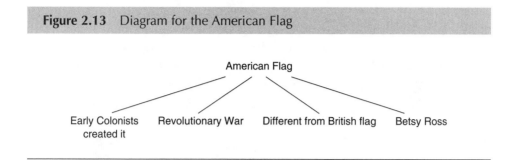

Figure 2.13   Diagram for the American Flag

The most familiar graphic to support students in comparison is a Venn diagram. This allows students to identify similarities and differences. (See Chapter 5 for an example.)

READING INFORMATIONAL TEXT TO LEARN ABOUT STRUCTURE

In the informal writing shared earlier in this chapter, students were writing about the texts that they read. The goal was understanding of content. Teachers can also use informational texts to serve as models so that students become familiar with their organizational structure and can use them in their formal writing endeavors.

All informational texts provide this opportunity for students to learn about their structures. We highlight just a few to show how explicit exploration of their structure supports student reading and writing of informational text.

Leveled Books

Casbergue and Plauche (2003) noted that many early-leveled books are informational. One example is the book *Orangutans* (Marchetti, 2001). This book is descriptive, with each chapter focusing on an important aspect of orangutans. The first chapter describes what they are, the next what they eat, then where they live, and the book ends with a chapter about their play. This book serves as an excellent model for young children's exploration of animals, plants, and so on. It provides a model where every page contributes one new fact about orangutans.

Picture Books

There are numerous picture books that focus on information. They move from simple to complex. Teachers need to consider these books carefully, as often they are very complicated and require teacher support, particularly for beginning readers.

One of the simplest categories of content area picture books is the alphabet book. We have many favorites in the content areas, but one of our favorite authors is Jerry Pallotta. He has informational text ABC books about deserts, oceans, frogs, dinosaurs, bugs, airplanes, and many others. The format lends itself to vocabulary development and writing in all the content areas. Another one of the picture books that falls into a simpler category is *Fruit* (Jeunesse & deBourgoing, 1989). This book is part of a series centered on first discoveries. *Fruit* begins with an exploration of different types of apples. It then considers the inside of apples. This part of the book is descriptive in structure. Once apples are described, the book then looks at other fruits. This is where the book takes on a comparison structure. While the book has two structures for students to explore, there is little text and a great deal of picture support, thus making it perfect for beginning readers and writers.

Other picture books like *How Would You Survive as an Ancient Egyptian?* (Morley, 1995) are much more complicated and, while having picture support, rely heavily on text. They could be used with beginning readers and writers only with direct support from a teacher. This book has multiple organizational strategies within it. It begins with simple description, but then it quickly moves to a question structure, where readers must find answers. This represents the problem-solution format. There are also opportunities for students to use this book as part of a comparison essay. For example, there are detailed examples of an Egyptian town and home. These descriptions could serve as a base for comparisons of other ancient civilizations or to a comparison with civilization today.

Chapter Books

These books are organized by chapters, are longer, and have minimal visual support. One example is *The Giant Germ* (Capeci, 2000). This book is part of the Magic School Bus series and combines narrative with informational writing. Students in Ms. Frizzle's class take field trips and explore science content. In this particular book, there are notes sprinkled throughout the book with facts about germs.

Michelangelo (Stanley, 2000) is a book that is totally informational. The book shares information about Michelangelo and his paintings. Its structure is predominantly descriptive.

Reference Books

This category includes textbooks, almanacs, dictionaries, encyclopedias, and other source books that provide information for student writers.

The majority of these are organized by description. While description is the dominant organization, textbooks such as science and social studies often provide students with sequence and cause-and-effect organizational structures.

FINAL THOUGHTS

Informational writing, both informal and formal, can begin with very young children. Most important, teachers need to be aware of the various ways that children write about information based on their current literacy knowledge and understandings. As shown in this chapter, Noah responded with a picture and one sentence about spiders. Kennady provided several sentences and one illustration. Other students with more literacy knowledge responded with full essays, as seen in Josie's writing. All of these students demonstrated that they were engaged with informational text and with writing about it.

Writing about information is best established in classrooms where students have daily opportunities to read, discuss, write, and explore. As was seen in the opening vignette, Jaryd and Eric formed a partnership where they researched together and shared information. They had the opportunity to explore numerous resource materials and to chat about their discoveries. Through this discussion, their individual research endeavors were strengthened in that they had a more complete understanding of the patriot they researched. They also had numerous opportunities to read, chat, write, and revise their information before sharing it with a public audience. This time to think and reflect was critical to their discoveries. It is important time that is often difficult to find in today's classrooms.

3 Writing Narrative

Vanessa:	What's the title going to be?
Denise:	"One Boy and Two Girls"
Vanessa:	That's not good.
Denise:	What should it be then? "The Man and Two Women"?
Vanessa:	That's not good either.
Denise:	"The Happy Scary Thing"?
Vanessa:	No. "The Thing That Makes You Shiver." "Things That Make You Shiver."
Denise:	No!
Vanessa:	"One Boy and Two Girls" doesn't make sense.
Denise:	Well, what should it be? I know what it should be called: "The Vampire."
Vanessa:	Ah, whatever you want. Wait! It should be "Be Careful What You Wish For."
Denise:	And a girl could say, I wish I was a vampire. And she could turn into a vampire.
Vanessa:	And the boy already was one.
Denise:	I wish I was a vampire.
Vanessa:	I said to myself on a star. NO, I wish to a star.
Denise:	Write yours! We won't have time to share. (Dyson, 2003, pp. 161–162)

Dyson (2003) documented this conversation as she studied how young children learn to write. Vanessa and Denise engaged in discussion as they constructed their writing. There was give and take as the girls determined the best title for Denise's story about vampires. There is also evidence in this exchange that the girls understood that boys and girls are represented differently in their stories—girls can become vampires but boys are already vampires.

NARRATIVE WRITING

This chapter explores narrative writing in elementary classrooms. It begins with a background of narrative writing instruction. The chapter then focuses on informal narrative writing. As with the chapter on writing about information, the chapter concludes with an exploration of more formal narrative writing.

Narrative Writing in Classrooms

The work of Graves (1983) and Calkins (1986) influenced classroom writing with the introduction of the writing workshop. The most notable difference that came with writing workshops was that the process of writing became as important as the finished product. Students were no longer expected to produce a perfect composition on their first draft. In fact, not all attempts at writing resulted in a finished product. Students were given the power to decide which early drafts of writing would go through revision and editing for final publication.

The Writing Process

The writing process that students work through during a block of time called a writing workshop involves five stages. The first stage is prewriting where students engage in thinking about what will be written. They brainstorm possible topics, their potential audience, the purpose for writing, and the form of writing (Tompkins, 1990). Murray (1990) believed that prewriting required the most writing time, in general about 70%. Following prewriting comes drafting. This is where students focus on getting their ideas down on paper. The main goal is ideas, not the mechanics of writing like punctuation and spelling. As seen in Chapter 2, as students develop in literacy knowledge and understanding, they are often able to compose first drafts and consider punctuation and spelling simultaneously. However, most young children are able to maintain only a singular focus. Either they write ideas or they correct spelling, but they cannot do both processes at the same time. Often if their focus shifts to spelling or punctuation, they forget the ideas they were trying to represent.

After a rough draft is complete, a student and his or her teacher decide if the draft should move forward in the process or if it should be abandoned. If the decision is to move forward, the student, with the help of peers and the teacher, engages in revision of this writing. Revision, as with the first draft, is concerned with ideas—their cohesiveness and completeness. Student writers also consider voice and the form of their writing. Following substantial revision, the writer moves to editing. This process is often jointly engaged in with a peer. Here the student corrects spelling, grammar, capitalization, and punctuation.

The last part of the process involves making a copy of the writing to share with others. This final draft should be as correct as possible so that other readers are not hampered in comprehension by numerous mechanical errors. Often, teachers have students word process the final draft, with the word processing program helping with spelling and grammar conventions. Sharing is done with classmates, other classes, and other appropriate audiences (Tompkins, 1990).

The Writing Workshop

Authors such as Graves (1994) and Calkins (1986) talk about daily time for writing and the organization of a writing workshop. The strength of writing each day is that students know they have multiple opportunities to come back to a piece of writing. They don't have to start and conclude each piece of writing in a single session. Teachers determine the best organization for themselves and their students so there is variability in structure in classrooms, but most workshops are half an hour to an hour in length. Typically, there is time for explicit group instruction, time to write independently, time to revise or edit individually or with peers, and time for class sharing. This rhythm of instruction is repeated in each workshop.

The expectations for teachers are that they provide explicit, systematic instruction to their students that moves them forward in their writing abilities. Teachers have multiple topics to explore, such as genres, voice, organization, and conventions. Atwell (2002) recently wrote about lessons that meet the explicit and systematic expectations and help guide teachers in providing meaningful lessons. In addition to this direct instruction, teachers record where students are in the writing process. Some teachers use charts with each student's name written on it—similar to a calendar where the days of the week are replaced with student names. As the teacher moves among students, he or she briefly interacts with them and gets an update of their current status. This is recorded so that when teachers next meet with students, they can ask about progress on this particular activity. For example, they might ask, "How is the revision coming on your story about football?"

Teachers also engage in in-depth conversations with students when they are revising work. These conversations can become complicated, as the teacher's role is to nudge the student to more proficient writing *without* taking over the student's writing. More details about revision are shared in Chapter 4. Another concern during conferencing with an individual student is the issue that the remainder of the class be productively involved with writing. Classroom management plays a large role in the success of a writing workshop. Teachers build student responsibility and independence in working without their direct support as they work with individual students. This process takes time to develop. Calkins (1994) recommended that periodically in a writing workshop, the teacher stop to take a status-of-the-class report. In this report, the teacher asks a few children what they are doing and how they feel about their effort. Once this brief status report is taken, the teacher goes back to working with individual students. This report lets students know their teacher is interested in what they are doing and expects that they are appropriately working on their writing.

The final expectation for a writing workshop is that teachers provide opportunities for students to share their work. Sometimes this sharing is a final draft, and other times students share in-process work to gain feedback. Sharing allows students to read their work to a real audience and thus learn how to read to groups and field questions about their work. Often when observing young students share their work, the only thing that is visible is a head behind a book. It is impossible to hear the words read by the student. Effective sharing so that others can hear is a process that is learned over time in classrooms.

WRITING DEVELOPMENT

Early Writing Development

A first step in learning about writing is taken by young children when they develop an understanding of the differences between writing and drawing. Harste, Woodward, and Burke (1984) observed young children as they scribbled, and they noted variations in their scribbling. Typically, by three years old, children used large scribbles for drawing and small scribbles for writing. Martlew and Sorsby (1995) observed that while young children differentiate these two, the boundaries between them are not fixed. Young children, even when they can more conventionally draw and write, use whichever form is most salient for the task at hand. This flexibility with written representation was also documented by Rowe (1994) when she observed a young child take a piece of paper and write on it, turning it into a note to another child, and then send it into the air like an airplane. Labbo (1996) described this same flexibility when young children explore symbols and objects on a computer screen.

Ferreiro and Teberosky (1982) demonstrated how these early explorations begin to be refined. They observed that children made a large mark for a big object and small marks for small objects. Or children will draw a long line for something that is big and a small line for something that is smaller in size. As children began to explore the abstract symbols of writing, they used size or length of their symbols to designate the object they were representing. It is easy to see how this strategy would be unsuccessful when they tried to represent an abstract concept.

Beginning Writing Development

From these beginnings with the abstract nature of the symbols or letters used in writing, children start to represent words with an initial consonant (Bear, Invernizzi, Templeton, & Johnston, 2000). They might spell *bear* as *B* or *dog* as *D*. This writing engaged in by beginning writers requires much more brain involvement than earlier scribbles or random letters for writing, as children are now connecting a sound to a symbol. When children who are using this strategy are asked to write, their text is often one sentence represented by a letter for each word. For example, a child wrote *ILTMAH*, which meant "I like to make a house." As might be expected, when children compose narratives using this strategy, the narrative text is short and, without the student's help, difficult to impossible to decipher. However, children learn that they are capable of communicating ideas in writing, and with teacher support these messages can be written in conventional formats so that others can read and understand them.

Developing Writing Development

When children are given opportunities to read and write, they soon add the ending consonant and then the medial vowel and are considered developing writers. A word like *sleep* might be spelled *SLEP*, as the child is using the *E* to represent the long vowel pattern of *E* in this word. Because students spend considerable time writing in this letter-by-letter way, their messages tend to be short, much shorter than what they can orally say about their writing topic. While their writing is easier to read than the writing of a student who only uses initial consonants to represent words, confusion is still prevalent, as the medial vowels are often confused. For example, the words *slip* and *sleep* can both be represented by *SLEP*.

Calkins (1986) noted that these children, beginning writers, most often write about themselves and their families. Frequently, their writing lacks needed details that a reader requires to understand their text, for they assume that the reader already has this background information. Often the illustrations that accompany these texts provide important details that did not appear in the writing.

Proficient Writing Development

Once students grasp representing single-syllable words and have acquired enough sight words that they begin to write whole words without intensive focus on each letter, their compositions demonstrate additional length and detail. Often these longer narratives are constructed with an *and then* structure, where students add text by repeating the phrase *and then* . . . (Calkins, 1986). Gradually, with much teacher support and explicit instruction, students move to more complex organizations for their writing.

These students, proficient writers, are also more purposeful in their writing and provide the reader with the necessary background information so that their text is understood. They also think about voice as they write and often include dialogue. Students explore various genres in their writing and begin to choose poetry, informational text, reports, plays, and so on for their writing endeavors. These students also show frustration with their writing when it fails to match their expectations. While less experienced writers are satisfied with a quantity of stories, these students have many false starts as they try to meet their personal expectations.

Once students have mastered short- and long-vowel single-syllable words, they move to understanding how syllables are added to words. They learn when a final letter has to be dropped, doubled, or left alone. When students are confident in their spellings of these more difficult, multisyllabic words, they become confident in their writing. They craft their writing, often looking for the perfect word or necessary detail. These writers spend substantial time with revision, as they appreciate a well-focused and properly organized piece of writing. They choose the best form for their writing, as they are well aware of the audience they are writing to (Bereiter & Scardamalia, 1987).

Understanding this development helps teachers know how to support writers in their classrooms. A writer who is struggling to find the correct representation of a medial vowel requires more support from a teacher in sharing his or her message. Revision and editing are done with the help of the teacher and are not often substantive. However, a student who can easily represent any word attempted is able to write more complex texts that go through independent, peer, and teacher-supported revision and editing.

GENDER AND WRITING

Gendered narratives are seen even in the writing of young students. Minns (1991) observed that young boys wrote about characters that had power and acted upon it. She shared one example of a young boy's writing about *Jaws* and how it attacked people. In comparison, girls wrote about friendship and support. Dyson's work (1995, 1996, 1997, 1999, 2001) shared similar results. She observed that the children she studied co-opted popular culture for their writing. Because of this, boys most often had dominant roles where they saved people from evil and girls were the ones to be saved.

In addition to topic choice, boys and girls have differences in their development as writers. White (1986) noted that by the end of the primary grades, girls were competent writers and also understood themselves as writers. Boys, on the other hand, were still developing their skills as writers and preferred informational writing over narrative writing. Similarly, Millard's (1995) research showed that girls wrote more complex, longer texts in the early grades. Their texts used a wider range of verbs and adjectives and included more elaboration. However, girls saw themselves as an observer in their writing, rather than a doer of the action when action was involved.

Moreover, young boys' writing is often considered to be disrespectful and unacceptable to teachers (Gilbert, 1989). Teachers are uncomfortable with the violent actions of the characters prevalent in boys' stories. This tension about suitable topics is often observed in classrooms as boys struggle to find classroom-accepted writing material.

These differences in the writing of boys and girls are important for teachers to consider. Students, as they explore topics to write about, are thoughtful about what is appropriate for their peers and teachers. While girls are more easily able to comply and find topics that please both audiences, boys find this more difficult. They are torn between male stories that are prevalent in the popular culture and how to interpret these narratives so that they find classroom acceptance.

INFORMAL NARRATIVE WRITING

Informal narrative writing is focused on idea sharing, rather than conventions. In addition to the informal writing used by teachers in content areas to clarify and extend student ideas, teachers utilize informal narrative writing to come to understand their students and to engage in written conversations about their reading. The most common form for this writing is in journals and reading response journals.

Journals

Journals are used for a variety of purposes in elementary classrooms. They provide a space where students can just put down ideas, thoughts, or feelings. They offer the opportunity for students to build fluency in their writing, for journal entries are a free form of writing where ideas are pre-eminent and conventions move to the background. As students become more proficient in their understandings of how words are spelled, though, they are also able to conventionally spell and punctuate as they produce first-draft writing.

Most teachers find the same time of day, each day, for students to write in journals. Typically, teachers allow students to write to their own topics and provide topics for writing as well. When teachers read and respond to journal entries, students build a personal connection with their teacher (Barone & Lovell, 1987). In many classrooms, teachers ask students to brainstorm possible topics for journal entries so that when they struggle to find a topic, they can refer to this personal list.

Teachers can also model journal writing to students by sharing some of the following books that have characters who keep journals. Two of the more familiar characters who rely on their journals are Harriet in *Harriet the Spy* (Fitzhugh, 1964) and Leigh in *Dear Mr. Henshaw* (Cleary, 1983). Figure 3.1 shares numerous book titles that have characters who keep journals.

Tchudi and Tchudi (1984) suggested possible writing topics for journals that explore students' experiences in and out of school. They suggested that students could write about

- Sharing past experiences
- Analyzing opinion to better understand personal beliefs
- Using the senses to expand on writing
- Recording impressions about people, places, and new experiences
- Responding to an article, television show, and so on
- Conducting a dialogue with someone

Figure 3.1   Children's Books With Journal Writing

Ada, A. (1994). *Dear Peter Rabbit*. New York: Atheneum Books for Young Readers.

Ada, A. (1998). *Yours truly, Goldilocks*. New York: Atheneum Books for Young Readers.

Adlier, D. (1985). *Eaton Stanley and the mind control experiment*. New York: E. P. Dutton.

Anderson, J. (1987). *Joshua's westward journal*. New York: William Morrow.

Blos, J. (1979). *A gathering of days: A New England girl's journal, 1830–1832*. New York: Scribner.

Cleary, B. (1983). *Dear Mr. Henshaw*. New York: Harper.

Cleary, B. (1984). *The Ramona Quimby diary*. New York: William Morrow.

Conrad, P. (1992). *Pedro's journal: A voyage with Christopher Columbus*. Madison, WI: Turtleback.

Fitzhugh, L. (1964). *Harriet the spy*. New York: Harper.

Frank, A. (1952). *Anne Frank: The diary of a young girl*. New York: Doubleday.

Goffstein, M. (1984). *A writer*. New York: Harper & Row.

Hesse, K. (1997). *Out of the dust*. New York: Scholastic Press.

Hest, A. (1994). *The private notebooks of Katie Roberts, age 11*. Cambridge, MA: Candlewick Press.

Hoban, L. (1976). *Arthur's pen pal*. *New York:* Harper & Row.

James, S. (1991). *Dear Mr. Blueberry*. New York: Simon & Schuster.

Lowry, L. (1984). *Anastasia, ask our analyst*. Boston: Houghton Mifflin.

Moss, M. (2002). *Emma's journal: The story of a colonial girl*. New York: Harper, Brace.

Murphy, J. (1998). *West to the land of plenty: The diary of Teresa Angelino Viscardi*. New York: Scholastic.

Oakley, G. (1987). *The diary of a church mouse*. New York: Atheneum.

Reig, J. (1978). *Diary of the boy king Tut-Ankh-Amen*. New York: Scribner.

Roop, P., & Roop, C. (2000). *Goodbye for today: Diary of a young girl at sea*. New York: Atheneum.

Shapiro, D. (1997). *Letters from the sea*. Arcata, CA: Paradise Cay.

Sharmat, M. (1982). *Mysteriously yours, Maggie Marmestein*. New York: Harper & Row.

Taylor, J. (1992). *Letters to children from Beatrix Potter*. New York: Frederick.

Williams, V. (1981). *Three days on a river in a red canoe*. New York: Greenwillow.

- Collecting words, poems, or riddles
- Making lists of possible topics

We have included several examples of journal entries, some with a topic provided by the teachers and others with student-selected topics. We also have examples from young students to older elementary students so that readers can see the variation in entries that occurs across grade levels.

One of the earliest entries comes from a preschool child who in her writing decided to use *cursive* to relate her message. It is not possible to understand her message, but it looks like it was a list, as she has checked

Figure 3.2   Preschool Child's Writing Sample

each row off (see Figure 3.2). Another preschool child chose a different strategy to convey his message. He drew a picture of himself and signed his work with his name—Noah (see Figure 3.3). The final preschool example (see Figure 3.4) is that of a drawing of a fairy and accompanying text, "The fairy picked a magic flower." What is particularly interesting about this writing example is that the writer put dots between each word as a way to mark the spaces between words. She was not yet ready to just leave the spaces (Morris, 1983). All of these examples came from the same classroom, thus demonstrating the wide variety of writing strategies used by children in a single room.

From these earliest examples, children develop writing knowledge, and their message becomes easier to read. The following examples share journal writing that was guided by the teacher. The first example is from Jed, where he is telling his teacher what he would like to do in first grade. He wrote:

Figure 3.3   Noah's Journal Writing

I would go on field trips every day and be nice all the time [spelling corrected].

She replied:

Where would we go?

Her response nudges him to reflect further on his entry and to carry out a written conversation with her about planning for the year. It also sends him back to his message to reread it before attempting his next entry. This rereading often leaves students puzzled about what they wrote and causes them to expend more energy on accurateness and legibility in further messages.

Figure 3.4   Journal Writing About a Fairy

Taylor, a fourth grader, wrote to her teacher's question of "What bothers you?" This question was put to students when they were experiencing numerous problems on the playground. Her teacher chose to use journals to help her solve this problem. Following is Taylor's writing:

1. I get bothered when my brother plays his instrument.

2. I get bothered when I am reading and someone turns on the TV.

3. I get bothered when I'm doing my homework and my brother is throwing my papers.

4. I get bothered when I have to go inside.

5. I get bothered when someone calls me names.

6. I get bothered when someone hits me.

7. I get bothered when I don't go to school [spelling corrected].

Her teacher used this response as well as the other students' responses in the classroom to open a dialogue about working and playing together in nonfrustrating ways.

A third example of a journal entry in response to a teacher's direction comes from Marcus, a sixth-grade student. At the end of the first week of school, Marcus's teacher asked students to reflect on the experiences of this week. This is what he wrote:

> Something good that happened this week to me is that I got a one hundred percent on a test. Yesterday, I had a good time at football practice. And something else I got a nice teacher. I liked the first day of school [spelling corrected].

After Marcus's teacher read this entry, she knew that he had adjusted to his new classroom because he decided he liked his teacher and he was feeling confident by achieving a 100 on a test.

These examples demonstrate how journals support personal dialogue between students and their teacher. They allow students and teachers to come to know one another more personally than can usually happen in oral conversations in a classroom full of students. They provide a real purpose for writing and for making sure that the message is clear and can be understood. As seen in the preschool examples, the student was necessary to help understand the message. As children develop literacy knowledge, they are better able to convey a readable message through writing.

Reader Response Journals

Reader response journals differ from the journals described above, as their focus is on having students write about their reading (Staton, 1980). They are similar to journals because this writing is first-draft writing and often exhibits conventional errors. They are also similar to the informal informational writing described in Chapter 2 because their goal is to extend students' understanding of the stories they are reading. Teachers often model a response before allowing students to write freely about the book they are reading. They might suggest that students retell, summarize, or provide a personal connection to their reading. They also use this writing when groups of students are reading the same book as a way to engage students in conversations about their reading before or after they read silently. Often teachers individual write responses to the comments students make about their reading. When this ongoing dialogue is a part of the process, these journals may be called "dialogue journals."

Following are examples of second- and third-grade students writing in response to their reading and their teachers' comments as well. In Figure 3.5, Nicole wrote about Ramona (students were reading various *Ramona* books by Cleary) making breakfast. Her response demonstrates literal comprehension as she just describes what is happening in the book (Barone, 1990). Another response to food in a *Ramona* book came from Jodie (see Figure 3.6). She chose a different way to respond; she used a double-entry draft format (Barone, 1990). In this format, the student copies an interesting portion of text on one side of the paper, and then on the parallel side explains why this text was chosen. Jodie's response is very different from Nicole's in that she is making a personal connection to text, rather than just retelling what happened. She is also responding to the comment written by her teacher.

Responses also demonstrate the varied interests of boys and girls or gender differences in responses. These two responses come from a group of students who were reading *The Egypt Game* (Snyder, 1967) in third grade. Mary wrote a letter to her teacher:

Dear Mrs. Jones,

Two girls pretended they were in Egypt. They took Egypt statues and pretended that they were real people. They used weeds for flowers and gave them to one of the statues that was supposed to be the god [spelling corrected].

Her letter response shows that her focus in reading was on the details surrounding the ceremonies that the children engaged in. Evan's response to the same bit of text in *The Egypt Game* is very different. He wrote:

When I read the book, it was weird because the strange guy owned a department store and on the top it said A-Z. And no one really knew the strange guy's name or what A-Z stood for. That's why it was weird [spelling corrected].

Figure 3.5   Ramona's Response

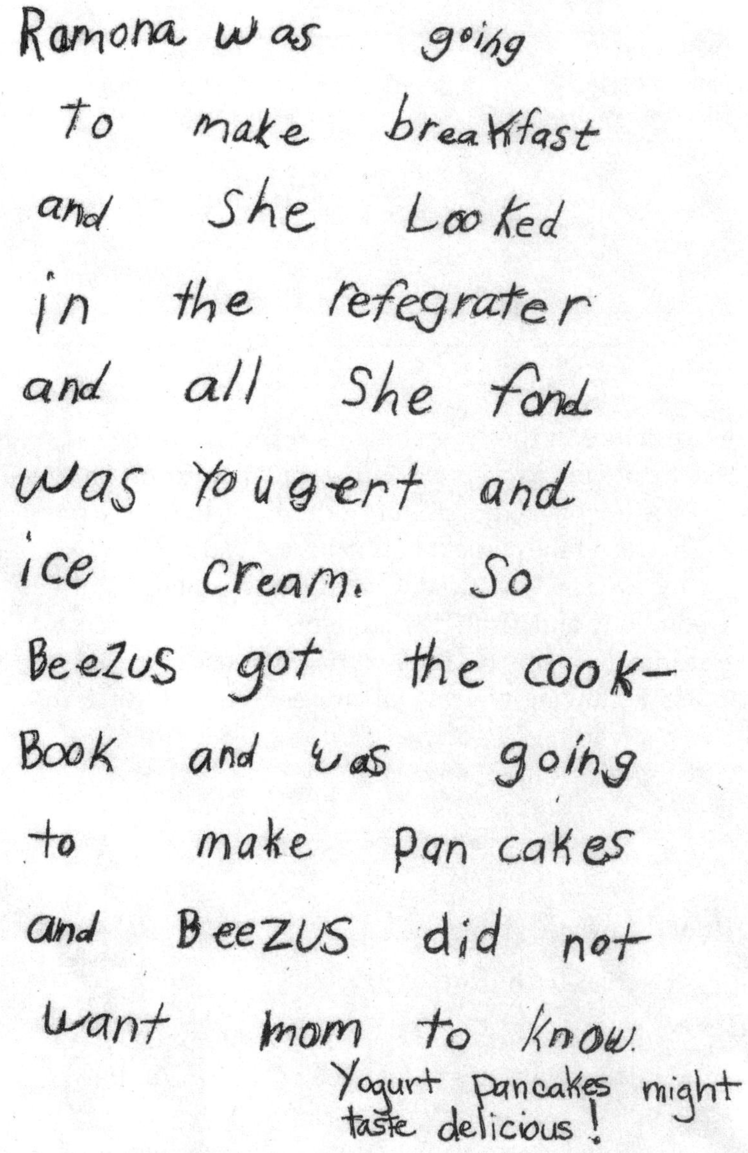

Ramona was going
to make breakfast
and she Looked
in the refegrater
and all she fond
was yougert and
ice cream. So
Beezus got the cook-
Book and was going
to make Pancakes
and Beezus did not
want mom to know.
Yogurt pancakes might
taste delicious!

His response does not just describe; he is trying to figure out what is happening in the plot. He is actively searching for evidence about this "strange guy." He knows that somehow he is involved with the plot of this book.

While the above responses came from students in classrooms where the teachers allowed them to respond freely to their reading, other teachers

Figure 3.6   Double-Entry Draft About Ramona

	D	E	D	
Then Mrs. Whaley said, "I hear my little show-off came in with egg in her hair."				It reminds me that I would never call my student that if I was the teacher. Do you think Ramona had her feelings hurt? Yes, very bad.

want more structure in the way students respond. Michael's sixth-grade teacher asked students to respond in particular ways on particular days. On Mondays, students wrote about vocabulary that was interesting or confusing. They used the context of what they read to try to figure out the meaning of the words. On Tuesday, students summarized their reading. Then on Wednesday and Thursday, students wrote connections to the text they were reading. Finally, on Friday, students made predictions of what might happen. Following are several entries from one week in Michael's journal. He was reading *Oh, Brother* (Wilson, 1988), a book about sibling rivalry, with a small group of students.

Vocabulary:

tempestuous—angry maybe

plentiful—maybe a lot of stuff

Summary—In the beginning of the book, Andrew takes Alex's bike all the time. Alex always has to take the bus. Then Andrew and Alex fight all the time.

Connections—I remember when a sixth grader told me to buy him some candy and he said if I don't he'll beat me up and I was only in the second grade at that time. Anyway I didn't do it and I ran away and told my mom. She told him to stop picking on me. Second grade was kind of hard because people wouldn't stop doing mean things to me. That's like when Alex ran into Mungo and I bet he was scared too. Just as I was. But Alex is in sixth grade and I was in second back then [as written by student].

> Prediction—What is Alex going to do to stop having his brother take his things? Maybe he will start taking his things.

The structure of these responses allows students to focus on difficult vocabulary and demonstrate a literal understanding of what is read through the summary. The teacher is pushing students to move beyond literal comprehension when he asks them to make connections and predict what might be coming.

Responses to reading engage students in reflecting on their reading so that comprehension is deepened. They also provide opportunities for students to develop their capabilities of expressing ideas through writing and then sharing them orally with other students and the teacher.

FORMAL NARRATIVE WRITING

Letter Writing

Teachers often engage students in letter writing, both business and friendly letters. Teachers often decide who will be the recipient of the letter. Students tend to produce more valuable letters when they know the person they are writing to and know that this is a real person.

There are all kinds of purposes for letter writing. Students might write to pen pals so that they learn about the circumstances of other students. They may write to authors or illustrators to ask questions about a story or text they have read. Or they might be asked to write to their teacher or parents to explain an upcoming event or the results on a report card.

Following are a few examples of letter writing completed by elementary students. In the first example, LaQuisha wrote to one of the authors (Diane Barone) to convince her teacher to let her help on the playground. Diane was doing research in the classroom and became familiar with all of the students, and LaQuisha determined that Diane could help her persuade her teacher. She wrote:

> Dear Dr. Barone,
>
> How are you? I'm fine. I got a new book. It's called "The Babysitters' Club." It's real title is "Kristy's Worst Idea." It said that in the middle, you should scratch a lucky flower to reveal how many free gifts you'll

get and how many you could get was 1, 3, 2, and 7. Mine said, "Surprise you get all 7 gifts free." My aunt bought the book for me and it cost $3.99.

I like Mrs. Schneider's class better because at math time I don't want to leave. I like helping Mrs. Schneider outside when she is on the playground. She won't let me hold the notebook. She tells me to go and play. I want to help her. Please talk to Mrs. Schneider so that I can help her.

Always,

LaQuisha [no corrections]

Her letter demonstrates that she knew the reader personally, as she wrote about her reading, a topic that Diane was researching. From this beginning, she wrote with purpose—the purpose of changing Mrs. Schneider's behavior. LaQuisha worked through several drafts of this letter before she distributed it. She wanted the reader to know what she expected and to help her realize a satisfactory solution.

A second letter was written by Anthony. His teacher expected that students write to their parents explaining their report card. The students brainstormed possible ways to explain their grades and how they could improve. Following is Anthony's final letter:

Dear Parents,

I did good in the first quarter. I got straight B's and one C. I am going to improve by not talking. No blurting out and when people are talking to me—just don't start talking. Those are the ways I will improve. The only thing I got a bad grade in was academic behavior and I got a C. Not talking should make that grade improve.

The things I am going to work on in math, science, and social studies are studying for the test, practicing my times tables, and reading more books. I want to get 100% accuracy on my reading tests. These are the things I will do to get more A's.

I hope you will like my grades this quarter. I will do better next quarter. I love you, mom. You are the best mom. You are nice and help me with stuff.

Your son,

Anthony [as written]

His letter, written for a real purpose, shows how he crafted it to demonstrate that he had a plan to improve. He also ended the letter by giving compliments to his mother so that she might better accept the results on his report card.

As can be seen in these examples, when students have real, authentic audiences for their writing and a purpose, revision and editing are eagerly engaged in. Students want their messages read and understood, and they do not want errors with conventions to get in the way.

Poetry

Poetry is perhaps one of the most difficult areas of writing for teachers and students. Teachers are often baffled at how to get students to write poetry. Tompkins (1990) recommends that teachers begin with poetic structures to scaffold poetic writing. She offers structure like *I wish* poems where every line begins with "I wish." Other similar structures are where every line begins with a color, a season, a sense, and so on. Once children are comfortable with these more formulaic poems, they can write more free-form poetry.

Figure 3.7 shares numerous books that can be used to model poetry as children begin to write it. Some of the books focus on poetic forms and others on word play.

One example of a poem comes from Josie. In sixth grade, Josie started to rework her narrative stories into poetry. Following is one of her attempts with the topic of space.

Space

In my room you see my brothers and sisters.

I always tell my dad, "I need my own space mister!"

I'm twelve years old and I need my own space.

I've got to kick them out then that's the case.

You never listen to me, can't you see I need to be free.

I'm a girl with power, a person who can devour.

"Please" let me have my own room

Or else, you will see me out the door soon [no corrections].

Figure 3.7   Poetic Books

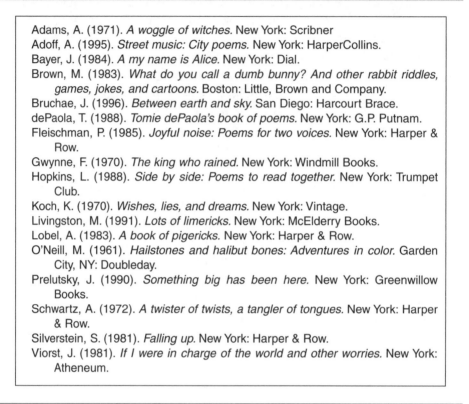

Adams, A. (1971). *A woggle of witches.* New York: Scribner

Adoff, A. (1995). *Street music: City poems.* New York: HarperCollins.

Bayer, J. (1984). *A my name is Alice.* New York: Dial.

Brown, M. (1983). *What do you call a dumb bunny? And other rabbit riddles, games, jokes, and cartoons.* Boston: Little, Brown and Company.

Bruchae, J. (1996). *Between earth and sky.* San Diego: Harcourt Brace.

dePaola, T. (1988). *Tomie dePaola's book of poems.* New York: G.P. Putnam.

Fleischman, P. (1985). *Joyful noise: Poems for two voices.* New York: Harper & Row.

Gwynne, F. (1970). *The king who rained.* New York: Windmill Books.

Hopkins, L. (1988). *Side by side: Poems to read together.* New York: Trumpet Club.

Koch, K. (1970). *Wishes, lies, and dreams.* New York: Vintage.

Livingston, M. (1991). *Lots of limericks.* New York: McElderry Books.

Lobel, A. (1983). *A book of pigericks.* New York: Harper & Row.

O'Neill, M. (1961). *Hailstones and halibut bones: Adventures in color.* Garden City, NY: Doubleday.

Prelutsky, J. (1990). *Something big has been here.* New York: Greenwillow Books.

Schwartz, A. (1972). *A twister of twists, a tangler of tongues.* New York: Harper & Row.

Silverstein, S. (1981). *Falling up.* New York: Harper & Row.

Viorst, J. (1981). *If I were in charge of the world and other worries.* New York: Atheneum.

Josie is trying to accomplish many things in this poem. First, she is learning about poetic structure; in this case she is using a rhyming format. Second, she is trying to persuade her father to give her her own room. Finally, she is showing her identity when she writes, "I'm a girl with power."

Poetic writing helps students focus on the importance of words. They must rely on a few, well-placed words to generate meaning. This is a tighter way to write that moves students to conciseness and precision.

Stories

Similar to their report writing shared in Chapter 2, students also compose longer narrative texts that go through the entire writing process. As students compose longer narratives, they learn about story structures like beginning-middle-end, repetition, plot, characters, setting, theme, and point of view. In addition to these structures, teachers inform students about writing traits. These include ideas, organization, style, syntax, and mechanics. These traits have been emphasized in other student writing, but because of writing assessments where the traits are scored following a rubric—where 1 is the lowest and 4 is the highest—teachers often bring students' attention to them as they compose longer narratives. The traits often serve as the focus for revision, where the teacher asks a student to improve a story by thinking about style, for example.

The first example of a longer narrative comes from Jennifer when she was in second grade. She drew a picture of several of her friends as a prewriting strategy. Then she wrote the following story:

> One day I was with my friends. Then another friend came along and she was mean to me. I told my friend but she got mad. She was being mean to me. Then one day that other friend did not play with us and we were friends again.

This simple story about friends demonstrates the *and then* strategy described by Calkins (1986). It is also partial in its telling, as we are not aware of the friends, what they are doing, and who actually is being mean. Jennifer assumed that the reader had this information and she did not have to recount it.

Another story written by a young student illuminates how the words *Once upon a time* are borrowed from heard stories to begin this story about a fairy. Maria wrote:

> Once upon a time there was a unicorn. A very lonely unicorn. It really wanted a friend. No one wanted to be his friend. But one day three fairies came to play. One was pink and one was blue and one was purple.

The story ends at this point. It had a strong beginning, and a potential plot was established. However, the story ended when the fairies arrived. There is no indication that they became friends in the writing; the author assumed this resolution.

Both of these stories written by young girls highlight the topics of friends. In both circumstances, the writer is not active but takes a passive role in the retelling of the story. These stories replicate the gender differences noticed by Minns (1991) in children's writing.

In the following example, Eric, during his sixth-grade year, wrote about being lost in the woods (see Figure 3.8 for the introduction to this writing). Eric developed a love for Gary Paulsen's books during this year, and his story is similar to Paulsen's where the main character is lost and has to use his wits to survive.

Eric's story, still not the final draft, brings the reader in immediately. There is action from the beginning, with Eric being the center of the action. Eric's voice is also strong in this writing. He allows the reader to hear his thinking.

These few examples share the development of student writers. Often their first stories are not kind to readers, in that much must be assumed by the reader. They then move to an *and then* structure where one event is tacked onto another. Then with the support of teachers and peers, students move to more complete narrative writing, as seen in Eric's draft. The focus is not just on completing a story but completing a story that has cohesion and organization, voice, a clear setting or settings, dialogue where appropriate, and correct conventions. This development is quite sophisticated and is predicated on daily writing with teacher and peer support.

Multigenre Writing

Romano (2000) shares a format for writing that includes numerous pieces that vary in genre. This collection of work becomes what is known as *multigenre writing*. Generally, once the pieces are written, students provide an introduction to the collection. As readers of this chapter, we might collect the examples of writing about friends and put them together in a collection. This collection might include journal entries, responses to books, poetry, and longer narrative pieces.

Another example of multigenre writing might begin with a book like *A Bat Is Born* (Jarrell, 1978). This book contains one poem that has numerous facts about bats. It begins:

A bat is born

Naked and blind and pale [unpaged]

A student might use this poem as the organizational thread through a multigenre paper. From this beginning, he or she could include information about bats that is found in textbooks, encyclopedias, and the Internet. Another piece might be a response to narrative books with bats in them.

Figure 3.8   Eric's Lost in the Woods Story

Lost in the woods

In the night while everyone was in their cozy beds, I was getting ready and head out towards the window. When I got out I saw this weird shadow. I followed the the shadow and it lead to this weird looking place. I wanted to know what it was so I kept following it. The shawdow left but I had found myself in a place where you could see nothing but trees. I was standing in the middle of nowhere surrounded by the dark green tall trees. I was so scared I was already regrating that I left home. I was getting real cold all I had on was my thin pj's. You can't imaggen how cold I was and how scared I was. I was so scared all I wanted to do was hug my parents and never let go. I'll tell them I'm so sorry for leaving home. I started to walk around but the dark green trees wouldn't let me see anything. I was real scared I was getting real hungry and ~~mark~~ colder by the minute. I hadn't eaten anything since I left. I didn't know what to do I was so scared.

This student might also create a graph that shows how bats are interwoven in these stories. He or she might create a chart showing the kinds of bats that exist.

Once these elements are in place, the student could include a narrative and/or a report about bats. When all of these pieces are combined, the student has a rich, detailed paper that includes fiction as well as facts about bats.

Other potential forms of writing that might be included in a multi-genre paper could be

1. Lists

2. Poems

3. Newspaper articles

4. Ads

5. Cartoons

6. Journal entries

7. Drawings

8. Charts

9. Interviews

10. Maps

The strength of these papers is that students can combine numerous sources and forms of writing to enrich the content. Each source adds an element not present in the others. For example, a list might identify the types of bats, while an interview might inform about how a bat is cared for. Each piece contributes to the whole report.

FINAL THOUGHTS

Narrative writing is the most prevalent form of writing in elementary schools. Teachers, particularly of young children, guide students in writing about their personal experiences. While writing narratives is an important accomplishment for students, teachers need to be cognizant of gender differences in preference. Boys may prefer informational writing and find narrative writing a challenge, while girls may prefer narratives and struggle with informational writing.

In addition, it is recommended that teachers balance the uses of informal and formal narrative writing. While journal writing is important, students need to value writing that goes through revision and editing. This writing is more difficult to sustain, as students work with a single piece over days and weeks.

4

Writing With Purpose for Real Audiences

Today's educators often view process writing as a relatively new approach to learning and thinking. However, as early as 1819, an editorial in *Juvenile Gazette* promoted writing as a means of reflective thinking for the young. "There is nothing better calculated to effect this object [thinking skills] than the practice of putting your thoughts upon paper. This practice will also improve your manner of expression and enlarge your acquaintance with the meaning of words" (Kendal & Johnson, 1819, p. 2). Indeed, process writing has its roots in a long, strained history between rote memorization for correct form and an emphasis on expression for content and meaning.

PART OF A CLASSROOM CULTURE

Mr. Cantrell looks around the room and notices that most of his seventh-grade students are still working on their morning quick write. Many have chosen to use one of the two suggested topics on the board, although a few are writing on self-selected topics. This morning he has provided two choices: (1) tell a story about something you learned this week or (2) tell us about a TV show we should see or a book we should read. Convince us we should watch or read it.

"About two more minutes," he cautions, as he adds his last thoughts to his own writing. He has chosen to write about something new he learned this week. He now knows that the Spanish word for accompany is acompañar. Because he has a large population of

Spanish-speaking students, he plans to use this cognate to demonstrate this connection to his class.

Travis already has his hand up to share. He begins to wave it back and forth in a dizzying fashion. Mr. Cantrell motions him to lower his arm so he doesn't distract any last-minute writers who are still finishing. He points to Travis and then holds up one finger to signal he will be the first to share today. Travis lowers his hand, folds his arms, and sits back in satisfaction with a smug smile on his face.

"Okay, now," Mr. Cantrell says after a minute has passed. "Who would like to read what they've written?"

True to his word, he calls on Travis first.

Leaning forward in his chair, a mischievous grin on his face, Travis begins.

"I learned about fungi this week in Ms. Jordan's science class. They have their own kingdom. Athlete's foot is a fungal disease in humans. I had athlete's foot last summer. I guess that makes me a fun-guy!" He laughs out loud at his own joke.

"Get it? I'm a fun-guy because I had fungi growing on my feet!" Several students roll their eyes as they chuckle with him at the pun.

Belinda has her hand up now and Mr. Cantrell calls on her. She begins, "Last night I watched this really old movie about these guys . . ."

Mr. Cantrell is providing his students with a focused free-writing choice of narrative-informational or persuasive-informational writing. He will note which preferences individual students are selecting to see if there is a trend and whether or not he needs to assist them in experimenting with a variety of purposes and formats so they are confident with all of them. He will also note which students are choosing their own topics and how they are progressing with a variety of genres and ideas to see how he can assist them in their efforts.

Like Jaryd's teacher, as described in Chapter 2, Mr. Cantrell uses writing as a means of sharing content knowledge and thinking processes. His students are often responsible for exit cards from his class with an assessment question to measure their understanding of the day's lesson. For instance, students might be asked to note the three most important ideas shared in the day's science lesson. In addition, he sometimes uses brief freewrites during class time to refocus students or to provide them with an opportunity to think about what they need clarified or to ask questions. However, his classroom climate is notable as one that encourages a variety of longer-crafted writing that is continuously developed and revised with frequent practice and experimentation. He balances informal writing with longer, sustained writing that includes revision and editing.

A classroom climate conducive to writing provides space to use writing for experimentation, to discover topics on which to write, topics that might not have occurred to the writer without the support of writing. In addition, it provides the freedom and respect necessary to learn by making mistakes and learning from them through revision, discussion, and an appreciation for the reader-writer connections. It is a classroom that helps students craft their thinking and writing through reflection and revision of ideas based on new thoughts and information.

WRITING FOR REAL AUDIENCES

Graves (1978) states that "children who are used to writing for others achieve more easily the necessary objectivity for reading the work of others" (p. 24). Providing audiences for children can be challenging and time consuming for classroom teachers, but we have found the benefits far outweigh the effort. Helping students understand and select the most convincing register and manner of addressing varying audiences is perhaps one of the most important communications skills that can be acquired through writing instruction.

Writing to Others

Letter writing is one of the oldest forms of writing instruction for young children. Lanham (2001) suggests that letter writing became the primary vehicle for writing instruction in Europe in the 11th and 12th centuries; and Benjamin Franklin (1749/1927), famous colonial U.S. statesman, in his instructions for teaching writing, suggested the following:

> To form their style they [students] should be put on writing letters to each other, making abstracts of what they read or writing the same things in their own words; telling or writing stories lately read, in their own expressions. All to be revised and corrected by the tutor who should give his reasons, explain the force and import of words, etc. (pp. 17–19)

As discussed in Chapter 3, letter writing is still a popular form of writing instruction today, although its form is sometimes altered to include electronic versions of synchronous (real time) and asynchronous (delayed time) networked communications. Its great appeal is undoubtedly tied to its prerequisite for a real audience. Letters are generally addressed to specific people with varying but authentic purposes.

In addition to the commonly used letters or notes of congratulations, sympathy, thank you, and get well to classmates, we have had success with pen pal letters between multiage classes, including letters between our preservice teachers and middle school students. Asking pertinent questions to find out interesting information about others and sharing topics of interest have provided both sets of learners with real audiences and purposes and also the promised reward of a return letter written specifically to them.

As elementary and commonsensical as it may seem, students of all age levels sometimes need to be taught not only the forms of letter writing but also how to frame a response. Through think-aloud models, teachers can demonstrate how to reply to a class letter with the original made visible for all to see. After thanking the correspondent for the letter, they can begin with the previous letter's questions and comments as a starting point for their own letters. Later, they can add new information about themselves and ask any new questions. Students can use letters as an opportunity to practice the wait time involved between completing apparent last drafts of writing to rereading the letter from the point of view of the receiver some time after the original is written. Then, by using point-of-view questions, they can revise accordingly. *What do you think the receiver will think and say? How will he or she interpret the whole message and its separate parts?* These questions and modeling are the beginning of early communications and revision lessons for the youngest writers.

Letter writing can also be used in combination with other lessons. For example, "Write to your teacher about how easy or hard the lesson was" or "Send an e-mail to the author stating what you want to know more about or about what was confusing." Letters to peers can be content-based, such as, "Write a letter to a classmate describing the process of division." It can then be reframed for a different audience (i.e., "Now write the same letter to a second grader describing the process of division"). Comparing the various delivery models, styles, and word choices is a valuable exercise in the necessity of revisions based on audience.

Letters home to family members can explain current or upcoming events at school. They can also describe learning situations that have occurred during the school day, hopefully ending the exasperating child-answer of "Nothing," to the parent-question "What did you do in school today?" Students can describe learning processes and content to inform parents and to stimulate school-to-home conversations and connections as well as demonstrate writing proficiency and areas for possible improvement (see Figure 4.1 for an example of a student letter).

Figure 4.1   Letter Home

Dear Mom and Dad,
    At school today I worked on my 6 times multiplication tables. I forgot $6 \times 9 = 54$. We played soccer at recess and Tim and I won the game for the team. I read a story and did questions about whales in reading. Tomorrow I need to remember to bring an old liter bottle for an experiment.

Your son,
James

Writing for Particular Audiences

Teachers are the most apparent significant audience for students. Report writing and assessments specifically directed at teacher audiences are covered in Chapters 2 and 5, respectively, of this book. However, there are other important audiences that direct young writers' attention to crafting a piece of writing through the revision process for more formal publishing or presentation. Some genres lend themselves to particular audiences. For example, in writing a speech of introduction or for an award, the content is aimed at all those listening; however, it is primarily directed at the person being introduced or congratulated. Having students write speeches of introduction, award, or thanks and then deliver them from notes provides publishing opportunities and a motive for revision.

Likewise, adding a dedication page to a short story or other piece of writing offers student writers a very different genre in which to write. It provides them with an opportunity to acknowledge, in a formal way, others who are important to them and, we have found, gives added value to the published student writing (see Figure 4.2 for examples of student dedications).

Two-way dialogues in script form or simply in brief conversational formats provide quick writes with real audiences who can agree and/or disagree with viewpoints, add to information or story lines, or converse in

Figure 4.2   Dedication

Example 1:
    This book is dedicated to my mom who helped me with the hard words.

Example 2:
    I am dedicating this story to my dog Sandy because it is about him.

note-exchange type of discourse. Teams of two can also act as interviewer and interviewee in determining which concepts or lessons they found most difficult or interesting in class and why. After writing out and revising these issues, teams of two can then combine and write interactively with other paired teams to communicate and share written perspectives on ideas with another audience.

Writing for Self

Examples of writing for a personal self-reflective audience, termed *expressive writing* (Britton, Burgess, Martin, McLeod, & Rosen, 1975, pp. 11–18), include journal writing, diaries, and any other writing that conveys internal thinking processes. (See Chapter 3 for journal writing examples.) Writing about a problem and including writing as an integral part of the thinking process helps students to slow their thinking for time to clarify thoughts, identify concepts, and refocus possible questions and solutions.

Predicting story lines, upcoming information, and writing questions while reading a piece of informational or literary text requires a thorough understanding of the information as well as the ability to organize, analyze, and synthesize reading materials. To connect with personal reading choices in a literary genre, students might respond to some of the following:

- One of these characters [name him or her] reminds me of . . .
- If I were [a character in the story] I would have . . .
- One thing I've noticed about the way this author writes is . . .
- The setting where this story takes place is somewhat like . . .
- Here's what I think will happen next . . .

Informational text also provides opportunities for reflective personal writing.

- The amazing part about this content is . . .
- I want to find out more about . . .
- This reminds me of . . .
- I wonder if . . .
- A related thing I would like to know about is . . .

Researchers (Rosenshine, Meister, & Chapman, 1996) found that "the practice of teaching students to generate questions while they read has yielded large and substantial effect sizes when experimenter-developed comprehension tests and summarization tests were used" (p. 189). These same questioning techniques hold promise for writers as well as readers.

Writing pertinent questions to study content material requires not only a thorough understanding of the material but also the ability to organize and synthesize information. For example, a student might query, "I wonder what I will learn about planets when I read this chapter and how I will include this information in my writing." From these broad questions, this student will generate more specific ones as he or she engages in writing about planets. After questions have been written, students can share and revise them based on their suitability as test questions and then organize and answer them to report on newly acquired content knowledge.

In writing for self, the craft of writing becomes an integral part of the thought process, a means of synthesizing information and self-monitoring thinking strategies to solve problems and create understanding. Students become not only better writers but also better readers and thinkers.

WRITING FOR REAL PURPOSES

Writing IS problem solving. The process itself is a series of decision-making choices about the content of the piece of writing and the form or conventions used to frame and communicate the ideas. This occurs initially and as part of the ongoing revision process. In addition, this problem-solving process of writing is a system for solving other problems by getting them down on paper for analysis and evaluation. For example, "Hmm . . . is this feeling a little like looking into back-to-back mirrors where you see several images of yourself coming and going?" Just as reading is much more than the process of decoding words, writing is a meaning-making activity, and it is important in generating ideas and questions, not just recording them.

Advice columnists have known for years that behind anonymity, people feel free to request information, even from total strangers. Setting up an advice or information box in the classroom with preset times to open and respond individually or as a class can motivate writers to solve real problems or seek and/or discuss information that might benefit the entire class. Students can submit items and/or the teacher can structure scenarios and issues for class response.

Advice columns can, of course, also be part of a class or school newspaper. Even very young students can write articles of interest and provide noteworthy news about their class or school. An example of advice for other students comes from a first-grade classroom. At the end of the year, each student wrote one piece of advice for next year's students. Eldon wrote: "Don't use pencils that are too short. You have sloppy handwriting when you do." The advice from all of the students was compiled into a class book to be shared with next year's first graders. With the ease of current desktop software and photocopying equipment, it has never been easier to offer this as a publishing opportunity for students.

In addition to news stories on events directly related to students' lives, newspapers can include editorials, book, movie, or software reviews, sports stories, and advertisements for events or fundraising activities. Our local newspaper provides a supplement each year filled with stories and articles from children. In one issue, students created ads for local businesses. One ad suggested, "Families should visit the Hilton where the entire family can have fun." And another recommended a local dentist for braces. By having this very authentic vehicle to share their stories, poems, and ads, students created a variety of writing genres for the public.

In addition to newspaper advertising, other formats for advertising provide students with practice at crafting persuasive text aimed at targeted audiences. Social and environmental issues are perfect venues for writing and producing public service announcements for even the youngest writers. Information guides are also ideal for purposeful writing assignments that can be shared orally during and after final revisions.

In addition, all types of how-to functional writing are appropriate throughout the curriculum. For example, in physical education, the explanation of an anticipated game includes numerous opportunities for revision of instructions and rules to ensure complete understanding of the procedures. One technique we have found especially useful in incorporating writing with physical education is to have students practice writing dialogue of positive comments to one another just before going out to engage in physical exercises and games. They are read aloud amid smiles and giggles during class read-arounds. But then, interestingly enough, with a bit of teacher encouragement we hear them again during actual participation in the sporting event. Other important functional writing purposes include instructions for completing art projects or a musical performance. These directions lend themselves to revision practice in completeness of details and organizational sequencing.

By writing and talking about techniques used for estimating in math, skimming and scanning in social studies, explaining scientific phenomena, revising a textbook account, or taking notes in all subject areas, students can share thinking strategies for these seemingly solitary tasks and discover additional tools for learning by listening to metacognitive "thinking about thinking" explanations by others. These types of writing can provide increased measures of academic proficiency when used over extended time frames (Bangert-Drowns, Hurley, & Wilkinson, 2004; Chambliss, Christenson, & Parker, 2003).

ANALYZING WRITING AS A CRAFT

Much can be learned by having students reread and analyze a favorite author's work. After a particularly engaging story, have students reread it and try to discover how the author crafted the story in such a compelling manner. Authors make many choices in writing. Through careful reading and discussion, students can determine where they might have made different choices, or maybe placed a different emphasis on a character or plot, or perhaps taken a piece of informational text in an entirely different direction. Atwell (1998) notes that early in her teaching practice, she urged students to avoid fiction as a writing genre. She altered her views later in her career, however, to include fiction, since that was the genre of the majority of her students' free-reading.

This tactic might be the way to meet the learning needs and writing skills instruction of students like John, the video games expert, or James, the class clown, from Chapter 1. Boys' literary choices that include action-filled violence often borrowed from popular culture like television shows or comics or slapstick humor are sometimes discouraged by teachers who perhaps fear the violent influence of such genre. However, allowing students control over topics can provide them with a semblance of control over their perceived out-of-control middle school lives (Newkirk, 2002).

REVISION

Mrs. Rivas demonstrates a revision process founded in cartooning for her students. She starts with a pear-shaped head, adds an egg-shaped, chubby body, and quickly turns the appearance into a caricature of a rabbit with oversized feet and large upright ears. She explains, "Like a cartoon character that starts out as nothing more than simple shapes, your first-draft writing, those first few sentences, are the beginnings of what you really want your readers to see when they read your final draft."

Graves (1978), in defining writing as "the making of reading" (p. 8), connects reading comprehension to writing by describing how the process of revision in writing forces the reader-writer to use higher-order reading abilities to refine and adjust ideas. Revision does indeed call on higher-order thinking skills as students read, evaluate, analyze, and synthesize by rewriting and reforming ideas.

Revision in this sense is much more than surface editing of precise wording or checking for compliance with a designated rubric. Editing, a separate but equally important process, is covered later in this chapter. Revision that is inexplicably connected to audience and purpose, to topic and genre, and to process thinking and writing involves guided lessons and much practice to master the craft. Writing, like any art, requires attention to detail and a motivated artisan with something to say to produce results. One of the important things about revision is that one lesson can impact student writing in a variety of ways. For example, a lesson on powerful introductory first sentences will result in a multitude of student interpretations. This is due to differences in student developmental levels in their understanding as readers and as writers. It is also affected by the specific writing events on which they are working.

Changing Viewpoints

Using familiar stories or other models and practicing revision through parody is one way to provide students with practice in the revision process. Having students attempt revisions of familiar tales can be entertaining as well as instructive. Familiar fairy tales, slogans or advertisements, and/or song lyrics are common material for student-written parodies. Another possible revision lesson with established models is practice with a shift to another character's version of a story. Children's author Jon Scieszka (1989) has created an entertaining version of *The True Story of the 3 Little Pigs* as told from the wolf's perspective. This type of revision allows student writers to practice with different perceptions of a topic as well as experiment with the craft of writing.

Revision practice from provided models can also be used by changing the point of view (e.g., first-person narrative, second-person persuasive, or third-person objective or omniscient). This most often involves additional adjustments in details and context to support the shift in person. For example, if the topic is breakfast, the first person "I" might talk about what "I" ate this morning, or the second person "you" could focus on what "you" should eat for a balanced daily breakfast, and the third person "he" or "she" could perhaps discuss what the majority of teenagers *don't* eat for breakfast. By changing the point of view, the topic and focus change accordingly.

Another way to practice with point-of-view revision is to have students interview and audio record a classmate about an exciting experience, then write it up as a story in the third person with a beginning, a middle, and an end. The storyteller could write the same story in first-person narrative and compare it to the third-person story version. In a follow-up discussion, students can note possible differences between the two accounts.

Changing Genres

In nonfiction writing, students might revise a memoir of *an unforgettable place* to a persuasive letter to a friend on why he or she should go there, or to a travel brochure about the sights and sounds available for visiting travelers. This type of revision encourages more than surface edits as students alter the focus, details, and/or wording in reviewing and rewriting a piece in different forms.

As explained in Chapter 3, multigenre writing is usually a topic-based or personal-experience-based assignment composed of several genres so that collectively they hold together as a single paper, but they can also stand alone as single complete pieces of writing (Romano, 1995). After students have been exposed to a variety of models and guided through writing in specific genres, this recrafting of a piece of writing into a different genre is a powerful tool for revision. Adding a prologue or epilogue to a multigenre piece is also a revision technique that can add insight into the process and enhance the writing as well.

Another variation is for students to write a postmodern story where diversions from the original genre occur along the way. Models of this writing occur in *The Jolly Postman* (Ahlberg, 2001), where letters, complaints, and nursery rhymes are inserted, or in *The Three Pigs* (Wiesner, 2001), where the pigs leave this story line and enter into others.

In addition, multisensory approaches to writing, where students are engaged in reading, writing, speaking, listening, and creating text together in a variety of production formats (e.g., letters, dramas, plays, advertisements, two-voice poems, biographical monologues, and/or video productions), provide engaging opportunities for crafting and publishing. Students can engage in this process singly or with a small group of students.

RESPONDING TO WRITING

Self-Check Responses

Checklists and instructional rubrics are ways to assist students in the revision process. Andrade and Boulay (2003) led students in an exercise where they helped them color code their first-draft essays based on criteria in a rubric to provide evidence that their work matched the defined criterion. They suggest that these self-check rubrics must

- Be written in language that is easily understood by students
- Include the criteria for gradations of quality work
- Provide suggestions for correcting common weaknesses
- Give assistance to works in progress to guide revision

Sometimes provided by the instructor and sometimes co-created with teacher and student input, these articulated criteria for self-assessment provide a starting point for students to begin evaluating their work and defining revision targets. (See Chapter 5 for additional information on rubrics.)

Checklists can also assist students who need ideas on how and where revision might take place. Checklist items should match the assignment or purpose of the piece of writing. However, here are some questions we have used to assist students in their first review:

- Does the opening or topic sentence provide important information on what will follow?
- Is there a better place to begin?
- Is each sentence clear? Will the reader understand it?
- Does each sentence contribute to the main idea? Is each one connected to the ideas in the other sentences in this paragraph?
- Do more details need to be added to support the idea or make the sentence better?
- Is the essential message apparent?
- Is there a better place to end?
- Are there paragraphs? If so, give a number to each and try them in a different order.
- Would this work better in a different form (i.e., if it is a story, could it be a poem, a play, a brochure)?
- Pretending I am a new reader to this writing, what will be my reaction(s) to the content? Would I be amused? Offended? Interested? Persuaded?

Peer Responses

As indicated by the purposes for writing in Chapter 1, being a good responder obviously depends on the ability to listen and ask good questions. Student response often requires much modeling and guidance to help groups eventually become independently productive. Teachers can demonstrate by using a student sample at the overhead projector and modeling the types of questions that might be asked. They can also role-play with one or two students acting as part of the response group and then debrief with the class about what occurred.

Students can also be provided with structures and models of questions until they are able to work independently in responding to one another's work (see Figure 4.3 for examples). Peer response groups can be author directed, with the author providing the questions and leading the discussion. They can also be responder directed, where the responding process is led by the responder providing his or her opinion, or in an interview with the author, as seen in the fourth example in Figure 4.3. They can also be done in a collaborative manner, where the author and responder share

Figure 4.3   Models for Questioning

Discussion leader	Opinion sought	Possible questions
Responder	Responder	Here are what I think are the main points of this piece of writing. Here is my one-sentence summary of the piece. Here is the one word in the piece that best summarizes it. Here is another word, not in the piece, that best summarizes it.[a]
Author	Responder	What picture do you see most plainly? What words or lines make you see them? What pictures do certain sentences (or stanzas) help you see? What parts do you like best?
Author and Responder	Responder	Here's what I see and hear. Is this what you mean? You know what I like about what you just read? It's this . . . One part I had difficulty understanding was . . . The very best sentence/phrase is . . .
Responder	Author	What is in this writing that you like? What is not there that you think might make it better? It sounds like you're going to . . . How are you going to do that? What are you planning to do next?
Author	Author and Responder	What is the single most important point? I decided on this writing format because . . . The next thing I plan to try is . . . The part of this writing that works especially well is . . .

[a]Adapted from Peter Elbow's *Writing Without Teachers* (1973).

opinions and compare perspectives. Practicing with a variety of questions and responses to student writers and then providing debriefing sessions on the processes and why they did or did not work lays the foundation for groups to develop their own formats for peer response.

The most common types of response involve questions about adding, omitting, or altering details, facts, or information to provide the best message. Responders can ask questions about parts of the writing where content is not as clear as they might like; they can suggest leaving out parts and help the author decide if the possible omission might alter the meaning or lose something in the style. By summarizing the essence of the piece or determining the most effective parts, they can also implicitly or explicitly suggest possible changes in emphasis based on the interesting portions or explanations.

To facilitate peer response groups, we usually pair partners or group threesomes with similar skill levels, and we insist on individual written response to each writer's work. This is for a number of reasons. First, by having the response provided to the writer in a permanent format, he or she can remember what was said and refer to it while revising at perhaps a later time. In addition, it holds peer responders accountable for providing valid feedback and also helps teachers in monitoring individual progress in learning the art of responding and in possible interventions when response pairs are not working effectively.

We have also found that the use of individual cassette tape recorders placed to catch the conversations of the group can later be played back by the teacher (we do this in the car on the way to and from work) to monitor progress and to provide feedback and assistance to productive and struggling groups. Successful models can also be shared by playing them back for the class the following day.

Student responders need help in developing a sense of empathy and good listening skills through frequent modeling, praise, and feedback. Writing-response groups need guidance in stressing and maintaining the importance of each student's right to be successful through a supportive and collaborative environment.

Teacher-Student Conferences

Teacher-student conferences provide teachers with valuable one-on-one contact with students that can allow for sustained, focused attention on individual needs. Together, teachers and students can discuss a range of text analysis from concrete mechanical aspects to the more abstract rhetorical components of a writing piece. Levels of teacher support range from those teacher-directed minilessons that occur as part of the conferencing session to a gradual shifting of shared responsibility to the student who becomes in control of the progression of understanding and implementing revisions through teacher-student interactions. Ultimately, the goal is student-centered direction of the revision process where the writer independently proceeds with revision after discussing possible changes with the teacher (Glasswell, 1999).

The student-directed conferences can be arranged in a number of ways. First, the conference can be specifically focused on an individual trait (e.g., organization) or on a newly acquired skill (e.g., using dialogue.) More often, however, students are working on a variety of techniques, and they can write out the two or three points they would like you to notice or on which they would like some advice or assistance prior to coming to the conference.

We begin with having students read aloud their pieces of writing while we jot down notes. Having students read aloud their own writing solves the problems of overemphasis on conventions; edits are left for follow-up assistance after the content and purpose are discussed. As we are busy recording the notes of what is said, the author is provided with wait time to search for the next thoughts or questions to be shared. These notes can later serve as a reminder to both the teacher and student of the aspects that were discussed.

Helping students to discover content, limit topics, balance text features, and explore what they have to say is the primary purpose of revision conferences. Sometimes by sharing colored markers, teachers can help student writers code topic-specific parts of a text and provide a graphic representation of possible disproportions or well-placed emphasis. Other times, the student is encouraged to invite one other classmate to join the conference because of his or her particular expertise in the writing topic or genre, and it then becomes a peer response opportunity with the teacher acting as one of the peer partners.

Record keeping for conferences can range from a brief note signed by both teacher and student that is tucked into the student's writing folder to filed notes (index cards or electronic files) for each student with the date, subject, and discussion summary.

There is a delicate balance between a teacher helping with the revision process and taking control of the piece. Because each student is unique and each student-teacher exchange is different and based on previous exchanges, the relationship is constantly evolving. Therefore, there is no set rule for how to conference with student-writers. Our best word of advice in knowing if the conference is helpful or if a different style might be better suited to a student is to ask him or her to assist in directing the conference content.

EDITING

Charles Dodgson (n.d.), aka Lewis Carroll, famed author of *Alice in Wonderland*, once wrote, "A great deal of the bad writing in the world comes simply from writing *too quickly*. Of course you reply, 'I do it to save *time*.' A very good object, no doubt: but what right have you to do it at your friend's expense? Isn't *his* time as valuable as yours?" (¶ 1).

Teaching students to understand and value their reader is the important message in editing lessons. While we have found that many students prefer to edit after they are done with final revisions, there are also those students who like to edit as they go. (These are probably the same folks who have a clean kitchen as they place the cake in the oven to bake.) Still others use a combination of the two. Students need to try all the methods to see which they prefer for different editing tasks.

By prioritizing the rules that are introduced and reviewed in class, teachers can provide students with self-edit checklists that can be used to assist in editing papers. We have provided a possible sequence of editing tasks in Figure 4.4. Although this list is obviously incomplete, it is a starting point for class instruction and demonstrates the large number of discrete editing tasks for which older students must ultimately be held accountable.

By introducing each rule separately in a brief minilesson and providing examples and opportunities to practice, students should be able to apply the rule in their own writing. There are, of course, particular editing issues that need to be dealt with on an individual basis for those students with distinctive and specific problems. For example, a student may experiment with dialogue in writing before an explicit lesson on quotation marks has been shared. Looking for and noting error patterns in students' work can help provide necessary information on the direction of future minilessons and how to group sets of students for instruction. This is especially important if some of the students are nonnative speakers who are not yet familiar with standard written English grammar and are negotiating between different language systems. By keeping track of patterns, not only will teachers be able to plan and provide appropriate lessons, but progress can be documented to show achievement growth. In the older grades, students can be responsible for and can keep a record of mastered editing skills in their writing folders; for the younger grades, teachers can use a variety of methods (e.g., a grid to check off mastery, anecdotal note cards, or notations on student writing folders).

Figure 4.4 Fifty Possible Minilessons for Sequential Editing Tasks

1. Capitalization: student's first name

2. Sentence recognition and development

3. Capitalization: first word in sentence

4. Punctuation: period

5. Punctuation: question mark

6. Usage: subject-verb agreement

7. Capitalization: names of people and places

8. Usage: some verb forms

9. Dictionary skills

10. Double negatives

11. Capitalization: *I*

12. Usage: *a* or *an* before a vowel

13. Usage: *I* coming second in compound subject

14. Capitalization: months and days of week

15. Punctuation: abbreviation of months and days

16. Punctuation: comma in complete dates

17. Punctuation: comma in letter salutation

18. Punctuation: comma in letter closing

19. Capitalization and abbreviations: St., Ave., Dr.

20. Capitalization: titles of stories, books, movies

21. Punctuation: series comma in lists

22. Contractions, using apostrophes: *they're, you're*

23. Punctuation: colon in writing time of day

24. Punctuation: exclamation mark

25. Correct usage of homophones: *to/too/two, their/there*

(Continued)

Figure 4.4 (Continued)

26. Punctuation: hyphen to separate syllables at the end of a line

27. Punctuation: apostrophe for possession

28. Paragraphing as new idea or change in direction

29. Punctuation: quotation marks

30. Punctuation: comma before or after quotation marks

31. Capitalization: first word of quotation

32. Paragraphing with new speaker/quotations

33. Punctuation: comma usage in combining simple sentences

34. Usage: *me* coming second as the object

35. Punctuation: colon for listings

36. Punctuation: comma usage in appositives

37. Run-on sentences

38. Punctuation: semi-colon

39. Punctuation: commas for groups of words in a series

40. Fragments

41. Punctuation: comma usage in complex sentences

42. Usage: pronoun/antecedent agreement

43. Usage: verb tense agreement

44. Capitalization: proper adjectives

45. Usage: correct pronoun case

46. Punctuation: comma to set off interrupting word or expression

47. Usage: correct adverb/adjective as modifier

48. Parallel construction

49. Passive voice

50. Common word confusions depending on student usage, for example *accept/ except, affect/effect, less/fewer, lie/lay, whose/who's*

WRITING WITH REASON

Comstock Elementary School is located within a cluster of similar schools in an urban area. The student body has a large second-language population, and most of the students receive assistance from the free and reduced-cost lunch program.

Today, Martha's class at Comstock is participating in a special writing activity. They are going out to the playground to "bury dead verbs."

"Hey, watch that shovel, will you?" grouches Martha. "Boys can be such dorks," she remarks offhandedly to her friend Tiana.

"Yes, well, girls are wimps," replies Matt, as he boldly levels the shovel over his right shoulder.

"Whatever!" retorts Martha, getting out of his way.

She is carefully carrying a cardboard box shaped to look like a coffin. Inside it, there is a list of verbs. They include am, are, is, was, were, have, has, had, and be, as well as any verb ending in -ing.

"Hey, tell me again. How come we're doing this?" asks Paulo.

"To make sure we don't ever use them in our writing," replies Tiana, staying close to her friend Martha.

While some of the students are unsure of the objective of the lesson, they all appreciate the outdoor break on this lovely autumn morning.

Ms. Hamilton is trying to teach her class to use vivid verbs in their writing. At a recent inservice class sponsored by her school district, she was introduced to the idea of actually burying a list of verbs to concretely remind students of those they should avoid. In the classroom she has a bulletin board displaying the same verbs as those in the coffin.

When they return to class, they take out their current writing pieces and begin to circle all the "dead verbs" they are planning to replace. They have written to the prompt: Tell about something you do well. It may be something you do at school or at home. Write about this so that your reader can understand what it is and how well you do it.

Luis, a limited-English-proficient student, asks Anaceli, who is bilingual, to translate and explain the directions for him and to help him understand the task. He looks at his paper and realizes many of his verbs, those he has been practicing with much diligence to master, are among the now forbidden "dead verbs."

Luis has written, "I'am Luis. I lik math. It's eazy and fun. It's eazy becaus is lenguage until I lurn english. I like math." He asks Anaceli what she thinks he should do about replacing the words is and am from the list of dead verbs on the bulletin board.

"Just use them anyway," Anaceli advises. "Why would you get rid of those verbs if they're something you didn't already have to begin with?"

Adam, meanwhile, is struggling to revise his sentences. "I am good at vidio games. One of my favrite games lets you kill bad guys with your powers. I like to kill bad guys because you save peaple." He carefully crosses out the "am" and smiles in satisfaction as he revises it to "I'm."

Tiana, on the other hand, has made good use of this language lesson. She revises her opening sentence from "I am good at babysitting" to "All the little kids in the neighborhood know, when Tiana baby-sits everyone enjoys the fun."

Today, there is a proliferation of rules-based, formulaic writing instruction manuals and inservice workshops being offered to well-intentioned but ill-informed administrators and their harried teachers. Although the teacher described above was certainly trying to improve her students' writing, the result was that writing became more complicated for her students. While a steady diet of *to be* verbs in writing is problematic, most writing includes their use. For instance, when was the last time you read a book or newspaper that was devoid of the above forbidden verbs?

Five-paragraph essays and power paragraphs proliferate as well as tips and tricks for the winning essay or high-stakes test score. However, like any one-size-fits-all model, they do not address the individual crafting skills necessary to acquire and maintain writing proficiency for each and every student. They are confusing the use of an academic form with the essential skills necessary to produce writing with meaning and purpose (Lane, 1993).

Making sure writing is an expected part of the day-to-day classroom culture is an important first step in ensuring student engagement with writing as a craft. Students must also be invited, enticed, and cajoled to try new, unfamiliar ways of expressing themselves, to craft in new written forms. Poems, fables, speeches, songs, fiction, informational bulletins, letters, PowerPoint presentations all provide the means of creating, crafting, and sharing meaning. And just as writers continually revise and re-see a piece of writing to craft it and make it better, so too do the best writing teachers continually recraft and revisit teaching practices to best meet the needs of their current group of learners.

5 Preparing for High-Stakes Writing Assessments

Mr. Buckley, building principal, arrives unannounced in Miss Farley's fourth-grade class on Thursday morning during language arts instruction. The students are completing a piece of writing on how plants contribute to the energy cycle within an ecosystem. Looking over the shoulder of Tanisha, he asks her for her graphic organizer. She explains that she didn't use one for this writing, although she does have a picture she drew as part of the beginning oral discussion. Mr. Buckley, obviously upset, approaches Miss Farley.

"Why didn't these students use the tabletop graphic organizer? Isn't that what the inservice class on preparing for state writing assessments told you to do?" he asks.

"Well, this lesson was all about sentence-combining activities. I had the children write sentences they could combine," she replies, somewhat bewildered.

"You are to use the tabletop method for all student writing. If I see writing in this classroom without the prescribed graphic organizer, I will have to take administrative steps to make sure you are doing your job."

He then turns to the class, smiling, and asks, "Do you know why we are emphasizing writing so much this year?"

"To pass the test," the class responds in unison.

> "Right!" he replies. "And do you know what will happen if you do well on the test? If you all pass the fourth-grade writing test? Well, I'll tell you. I'll throw you all a big party and we can celebrate your success!"
>
> The class cheers and Mr. Buckley leaves, satisfied that he is fulfilling his role as instructional site leader.

Mr. Buckley is responding to the pressures placed upon him in a climate of mandated accountability based on single-sample writing assessments, often in a high-stakes environment. Believing he needs a *quick fix* and not sure just how to accomplish this, he has brought in a staff presentation where a teacher, whose test scores rose last year, shared some techniques that she believes worked with her students. He is now intent on having his teachers replicate those practices immediately and intensively in their instruction to ensure increased proficiency at his own school site.

Today, writing assessment has become a dominant aspect of education with the federal testing under the direction of the National Assessment of Educational Progress (NAEP), state assessments sometimes as part of state accountability reporting system, and also some district assessments, all driving the urgency for proficient written composition examples as produced in test-taking situations.

HISTORICAL PERSPECTIVE

The advent of writing assessment as a widely accepted educational procedure predates our colonial era. Then, the composing elements under observation were evaluated according to Lindley Murray's *English Grammar* (1795/1825) and included instruction on concise and accurate use of words, phrases, and sentences under the subheadings of purity, propriety, precision, clearness, unity, strength, and the proper use of figurative language. Students were provided with instruction on clear sentence construction, unity, strength, and figures of speech in writing and with proper and effective word and phrase choice.

Writing as a means of assessing other content knowledge appeared in the United States as early as the mid-19th century. Prior to the 1840s, a school committee would annually visit each school, most of which were rural at the time, and present oral questions to the students on all subject areas, arbitrarily selecting from among the individual students for an oral recitation of the answers. The difficulty in this system is obvious. First, it was impossible to gauge who knew what. As luck would have it, a student could receive the one question he or she did or did not know. The tests provided a superficial view of what the class collectively and individually really did understand about the curriculum content. In addition to problems of equity and lack of useful evaluative information, committee members were sometimes accused of *playing favorites* by calling on friends' children for the easiest answers and on rivals' children for the more difficult ones (Caldwell & Courtis, 1925/1971). As a result, in 1845, Boston grammar and writing schools eliminated these annual arbitrary recitations in favor of individual written examinations. The written tests, they decided, were able to provide a more consistent and equitable system by which to determine the individual and collective proficiency of all the students as well as a viable means to compare one year's class with another (Caldwell & Courtis, 1925/1971).

Three levels of questions, recognizable today, were applied in written examinations in the past: (1) memory or skill, (2) intermediate, and (3) thought. Memory questions were those that could be answered by direct statements of fact, usually provided in the text. Intermediate questions required summarization or generalization of facts, and thought questions required application of information to new situations (Caldwell & Courtis, 1925/1971).

The dilemmas involved in accurately scoring student writing were difficult issues then as they are today. On October 15, 1844, and April 28, 1846, the *Salem Gazette* (Butler, 1935/1969) described a *point system* for determining proficiency in composition studies among other content assessments for first and second classes in the Salem Grammar School. For the grammar portion, the School Committee required the following:

> At commencement of the exam, a subject shall be given out for an exercise in Composition, to be written by each scholar upon the slate. Each exercise as thus prepared shall be examined in reference to the following particulars, viz.:
>
> 1. Composition to be marked from 0 to 10.
>
> 2. Proper use of Capital Letters from 0 to 5.
>
> 3. Correctness of Spelling to be marked 10, if correct, and one less for every error.
>
> 4. Punctuation—the same.
>
> Each scholar will also be required to parse three words (to be selected from the composition prepared by the Scholar) and to

answer three questions having relation to such portions of the Grammar as are required to have been studied by the class. For each word parsed right, and each question answered right the mark shall be 1; and for each error or failure the mark shall be 0. (pp. 314–315)

The written examinations promised to give a clearer picture of student progress and proficiency, but they also necessitated writing proficiency and instruction in all content areas. This procedure became the most common method of student assessment in the late 19th and early 20th centuries and had implications for curricular planning as well as for an evolving assessment system.

During the 19th century there was also evidence of teacher dissatisfaction with the amount of time devoted to content review and test administration from the lower grades through the high schools, with written examinations as often as monthly or quarterly, but typically "at the end of each term, or three times a year" (Lathe, 1889, p. 452). Additional criticism was focused on the competition perpetuated by the examination process and reporting. "The rivalry engendered is belittling; the ambition is low; the motive is contemptible, and teachers should be ashamed to set it before their pupils or to preserve a discreet silence upon it" (Lathe, 1889, p. 454).

With the intensification of the *scientific movement* in the early 20th century, more quantifiable approaches to evaluating writing were created. Dr. Joseph Rice introduced the scaling system beginning in 1903, using a five-point scale (100, 75, 50, 25, and 0) to rank student papers as excellent, good, fair, poor, and failure. Perhaps the most famous of writing evaluation systems was the one made popular by Edward L. Thorndike and George Hillegas, commonly known as the Hillegas scales. Educational researchers (Ballou, 1916; Breed & Frostic, 1917; Hudelson, 1923; Leonard, 1925; Trabue, 1917; Van Wagenen, 1921; Willing, 1918) continued through the next decades to offer collections of ranked composition examples on the basis of form and content. Using the graded writing samples, teachers only needed to match their own students' writing with the graded examples to determine a uniform grade. These types of scales for comparison continued to be popular up to the 1970s (Fagen, Cooper, & Jensen, 1975). Some of the obvious problems with using them were the variations in topics, modes of discourse, and the developmental levels of student groups, not to mention the teacher time involved in the process. Comparisons were not only difficult and time consuming, but also not reliable in many instances.

On the basis of ease of administration and reporting, as well as cost efficiency, standardized, multiple-choice tests in grammar and usage were often used as objective measures of student writing achievement during the 1940s and 1950s (Freedman, 1993). Although they often assessed only editing skills, these indirect measures were remarkably accurate in their predictions of student writing performance (Applebee, 1994).

During the 1960s, the use of direct writing assessments became popular. In direct writing assessments, students write in response to an assigned topic or prompt, and papers are scored by teacher-raters who have received training in the use of a predetermined rubric or set of criteria. The National Assessment of Educational Progress (NAEP) program began assessing student writing according to this method during the 1969–1970 school year. Over the years they have experimented with a variety of alternative objective and holistic methods for evaluating student writing, including tallying the length of t-units (independent clauses and their modifiers) and analyzing the types of arguments used in persuasive writing (Applebee, 1994). Today, they assess 4th-, 8th-, and 12th-grade student writing with direct writing assessments using a national random sample population. For more information on NAEP assessments, visit their Web site at http://nces.ed.gov/nationsreportcard/about/.

Individual states, and in some cases individual districts, also administer direct writing assessments to gauge student achievement across various grade levels, using holistic systems and rubrics to evaluate student writing. These are often included in state accountability reporting systems.

Some of the challenges for test makers in these assessments are the development of authentic topic choices that are equitable and provide equal access to all participants; the effects of time restraints on all students, especially second-language learners; allowances for the variations that different forms of writing can produce; as well as other reliability issues such as the test setting, which in many ways can be artificial in comparison to classroom writing or even functional writing as practiced in the world outside the classroom.

WRITING ASSESSMENT METHODS

Objective Methods of Writing Assessment

Objective writing assessments measure discrete aspects of writing such as verb tense, sentence structure, grammatical usage, and vocabulary in a multiple-choice format.

Similar quantitative measures, available with computer software programs, can count words, characters, sentences, and paragraphs; average characters per word, words per sentence and sentences per paragraph; and also provide readability data. Some will additionally provide the number of spelling errors and possible grammar errors per page, t-unit length, and proportions of simple to complex sentences. Many educators question the validity of these types of assessments. They are not convinced that these tests can best evaluate student achievement. They prefer the direct method of performance-based writing as evaluated with holistic methods because this type of assessment is tied more directly to instruction and provides practical applications to student learning.

Direct Methods of Writing Assessment

Direct methods of writing assessments deal with the actual production of student writing as the basis for a performance test. Students are provided with a set of instructions and some type of prompt to generate writing, such as a focused topic or question, a picture, or some other type of material to stimulate writing. They are given considerable freedom within which to create a written response. Papers are read and evaluated by specially trained readers, and each piece of writing receives one or more numbered scores based on an established set of criteria to indicate a level of proficiency.

Focused holistic scoring, *primary trait* scoring, *multiple trait* scoring, and *portfolio assessments* are all terms used to define holistic methods in evaluating written compositions. Different methods are often better suited to different evaluative purposes, and variations of each appear in national, state, district, and classroom-based assessments.

Focused Holistic Scoring

As early as the 1920s, researchers (Hosic, 1929; Hudelson, 1923; Lyman, 1929) warned that, like art and music, a piece of writing could not always be judged by the sum of its individual parts. In focused holistic scoring, evaluators base their judgments on each piece of student writing as a whole, separating out aspects or parts of the text and then combining those in a general overall impression for one score based on the quality of the written piece (White, 1985). Factors such as topic treatment, rhetorical methods, word choice, and conventional usage are considered as they work together for a relative total effect. A scaled rubric is provided, with point values matched to descriptors, and exemplary models, often termed *benchmarks*, representing each score.

Primary Trait Scoring

This focused form of holistic scoring uses scoring guides based on writing type—narrative, expository, persuasive, or expressive—and akes into account the audience, purpose, and task involved in the assessment. The scoring guide includes a copy of the writing task, criteria based on expected student responses, an explanation relating the primary trait and the task, a rubric of point scores, and annotated sample papers (Lloyd-Jones, 1977). It is especially useful in scoring writing where in-depth information is needed in evaluating specific skills in a particular writing style or in evaluating mastery of some specific content area knowledge. See the section on constructed response items later in this chapter for a set of scored student examples based on primary trait scoring.

Multiple/Analytic Trait Scoring

Multiple trait assessment provides separate scores for more than one aspect or trait on a single piece of writing. Using a continuum of relative quality for each targeted aspect of a piece of writing, it differs from the specific criteria used in primary trait scoring methods. Different analytic models focus on various factors, for example, ideas, details, purpose or focus, organization, wording or vocabulary, flavor, sentence and syntax, usage, punctuation, spelling, and handwriting, with some traits occasionally being weighted more heavily than others (Wolcott & Legg, 1998). The advantage of this system is its diagnostic value in providing more precise feedback to the writer about specific strengths and weaknesses of the paper. By evaluating content apart from conventional form, students can focus on each trait separately. The best-known trait scoring methods used today are variations derived from the six-trait writing assessment model developed in the 1980s at Northwest Regional Labs. For further information, visit their Web site at http://www.nwrel.org/ assessment/.

Portfolio Assessments

Portfolio collections of student writing extended over a period of time, although normally employed as an instructional tool, can also be used for assessment. Portfolios may take different forms depending on purpose and audience and can be a part of other content area instruction besides English or language arts. While some are geared to internal assessment directed by the student's own selections, revisions, and reflections, others can be used for external assessments by outside evaluators; those, however, must necessarily include standardized entries based on assessment purposes. Some progress through a semester, and others are spread out over several school years. Grading procedures and evaluation protocols need to be set up prior to initial selections to assist students in choosing samples. Collaborative planning and discussions among teachers and students are necessary to ensure that goals and procedures are clearly understood. The advantages of portfolio assessment are in the comprehensive collection of student work that reflects instruction and learning.

WRITING ASSESSMENT TASKS

There is a continuum of types of writing assessment tasks used in both classroom-based and standardized direct method testing programs today. At the farthest end is divergent writing, where students are allowed to select a topic and form of writing, take it through several processes and revisions, and submit it once it is ready for evaluation. In portfolios, students are sometimes encouraged to experiment with a variety of topics and forms to learn the craft of composing each. In standardized tests, this divergent type of writing prompt may provide students with open-ended directions such as, "Describe a favorite place" or "Tell about something you do well." (See Chapter 6 for student examples of this type of writing.) This type of writing assignment gives much latitude for student responses in hopes of providing a uniform yet stimulating topic. Test makers strive to ensure uniformity from prompt to prompt; however, although similar sounding topics may give the appearance of equality, the skills required in composing may often not be the same.

The other type of response is the convergent, topic-centered response that measures student content knowledge. Test makers refer to these types of test problems as *constructed response items,* and some states are using them to measure student proficiency in state standards including content areas such as math and science as well as in reading. They can be as narrow as "Name the two principal elements in water," or more broadly framed, as in "Provide three important causes for World War I and tell why you believe they are the most important." The continuum between these two examples of writing tasks includes varying levels of topic control between test writers or teachers and students, with the midpoint containing much shared responsibility for developing and expanding the type of writing. This is the on-demand type of writing used in many proficiency tests in addition to selected-response or multiple-choice items. Test makers work hard at writing these types of items to reflect state content and performance standards, and they generally reserve these items, which are sometimes multipart questions, for responses that draw on higher-level thinking skills.

HELPING STUDENTS WITH TRAIT-SCORED DIVERGENT AND CONVERGENT ASSESSMENT ITEMS

Miss Farley watches her students as they silently read the writing prompt before them. They have practiced for this writing assessment for most of the school year. She watches Tanisha methodically begin a graphic organizer, very linear, with numbers and bullets. Good girl, she thinks to herself. Keep going. You'll do fine. Kayla, on the other hand, is still sitting with a blank paper in front of her, biting on the end of her eraser, but she seems to be concentrating. I wonder if she needs help understanding any of the words in the prompt, *Miss Farley thinks to herself. Across from Kayla, Michael is writing away.* I hope they can read his writing. His ideas will be good and he'll score well if they can just read it.*

Todd, meanwhile, is done. In seven minutes, he has completed the assignment and begins to tap his pen impatiently on the desk, knowing he will have to wait for 50 more minutes for the rest of the class to be finished. Miss Farley catches his eye and makes a circling motion with her hand, indicating he should go back and check his work. He sighs, picks up his paper, and in a brief 15 seconds, rereads and revises his short composition, assuring himself that he is indeed done; he has added a period to the end of the writing.

Divergent Writing Assessments

Divergent writing tasks, designed to measure students' abilities to compose written text, allow writers varying degrees of flexibility in selecting their own topics on which to write. Often part of a writers' workshop approach to writing instruction, some pieces of writing are totally student selected in terms of topic and genre. However, others are sometimes based on teacher suggestions or prompts that can be narrowed to fit personal interests or to provide practice in form and content. Student writers work on different phases of process writing: prewriting, drafting, revising, editing, and publishing to communicate thoughts in an organized and interesting manner using standard conventions for readability.

Topics for standardized writing assessments intended for divergent responses are usually narrative, informative, or persuasive. (See Appendix for sample writing prompts.) Scoring rubrics for narrative and informational writing address the need for well-developed ideas and information, well-organized writing with clear transitions, a variety of appropriate word choices and sentence structures, and control over grammar, spelling, and punctuation usage. Persuasive writing rubrics focus on the importance of writers' being able to take a clear position that they can then support with well-chosen details, reasons, or examples. They too address the importance of clear organizational frameworks, specific word choice, and varied sentence structures, as well as few errors in spelling, grammar, and punctuation.

In providing instruction in the elements of good writing, a large number of teachers today use an analytical approach. That is, they focus on discrete elements with models, instruction, and student practice to accommodate student learning. Many teachers have been trained in writing process methodologies and the six traits of writing instruction, made popular in the 1980s and 1990s. This approach was led by Vicki Spandel and Ruth Culham (1994) and their teacher-friendly use of popular picture books to model and link assessment with instruction. Others prefer the concise and helpful four traits offered by Portalupi and Fletcher (2004) or Tompkins (2004). However, the important features on which to focus in a divergent writing assessment situation are always the ones being used by the test writers. It is important to help students by previewing and understanding the standards and the rubric to which they will be held accountable.

Total point ranges in scoring rubrics vary among test makers. The rubric carries six levels of achievement: 6 is excellent, 5 is skillful, 4 is sufficient, 3 is uneven, 2 is insufficient, and 1 is unsatisfactory. Some states use a five-point scale and others use four, but they all include some level of minimum score to indicate proficient levels of writing.

While specific rubrics vary among testing sites, they all include many of the same elements, which are ideas and/or focus, design and/or organization, language and/or style, sentence fluency, and standard conventions. These qualities do not occur in a linear manner in a writer's thinking (what does?), and they overlap and recur with varying amounts and intensity depending on the writer and the piece of writing. Therefore, writing is a reflection of student thinking in all content and social areas of the curriculum.

Ideas/Focus/Content

Quality, not quantity, is the central feature of good idea development. It is using precise information with specific details in just the right place(s) that make for an excellent piece of writing. Using a sample prompt, in whole or small groups, helps students to carefully understand and explain what the prompt might be asking and what best strategies could be used in collecting important details and responding. Students can experiment with a variety of prewriting tactics: clusters, lists, word associations, drawings or diagrams, self-talk, freewrites, and so on, so that a selection of methods will be available to produce ideas. They need to write and talk about which ones work best for different situations and for different learning styles. Practicing with lots of writers' tools will ensure they have some at their disposal when needed.

Design/Organization

This is often the trait that provides the most difficulty for students. Once ideas are generated and main points are determined, students need assistance in learning how to use various organizational patterns (i.e., time or spatial orders or most/least important to begin their writing drafts). Techniques for framing their ideas once the order is established can be demonstrated by modeling the use of outlines, arrows, color coding, numbering, or Post-it sorting. Graphic organizers can help build the framework of the piece. Some students benefit with practice using concrete visual organizers for reasons or ideas, including the *hamburger paragraph* and the five-part essay. Students need practice with a variety of appealing introduction styles as well as formats for satisfying and complete conclusions.

Language/Style/Voice

An understanding of appropriate diction and style for audience and purpose are a part of language and style, as is the individualistic, expressive flair that demonstrates ownership of a piece of writing. Writers with style show strong awareness of audience and can purposely use language to influence the response of the audience. Students need to practice using vivid word choices and to show rather than tell readers about ideas.

Sentence Fluency/Syntax/Sentence Structure

Partly a matter of style and partly a matter of convention, sentence fluency and syntax instruction connect the pattern or structure of word order in sentences, clauses, and phrases with the grammatical rules governing sentence construction. The objective is to produce a variety of fluent, rhythmic sentence patterns. Student practice consists of constructing and combining complex sentences and paragraphs from basic sentences to communicate fuller meanings and to avoid the repetitiveness of equally brief simple sentences or consistently long complex and/or compound sentence variations.

Standard Conventions

Students can benefit from instruction in how to silently *read aloud* their pieces to listen for errors or irregularities in their writing. Proofreading strategies can be shared and practiced, that is, reading for only one type of error such as punctuation at a time, or reading from the end to the beginning, or isolating one section at a time for careful perusal. For many assessments, students may make corrections on the original drafts of their writing tests, provided they are done neatly and legibly. This is important during a timed writing assessment, as there is often not sufficient time to copy over when an additional error is discovered.

Trait Bookmarks

Using the identified traits in reading and writing practice helps inform all areas of language arts as well as the other content areas. Bookmarks can be designed, exemplifying each trait, and introduced in reading and listening or writing and speaking exercises and then reinforced within the other(s). (See Figures 5.2 and 5.3 for annotated and blank bookmark models.)

Figure 5.1 lists some teaching and learning practices we have used with the bookmarks.

Convergent Writing Assessments

In convergent writing tasks, writers are expected to provide similar responses to items. They may range from dictation, with no choices in what should appear on their papers, to somewhat more flexible responses that call for logical inferences based on provided information or on content knowledge. Readers are intent on the relevance of the answers as they pertain to the information asked for in the item. The general features of writing such as vivid details, style, sentence fluency, or standard conventions are not under consideration except in their relation to the readability of the writing. If scorers cannot understand what the writer is attempting to say because of spelling, syntax, or carelessness in handwriting, an answer can be unintentionally marked as incorrect.

Convergent writing, that is, writing to a particular test item with expected right answers, is best evaluated with primary-trait assessment tools. It is not usually based on literary texts and personal perspectives, as is a great deal of current classroom instruction (Duke, 2004; Stotsky, 1995), but rather deals with informational text in a way that measures content and processes knowledge within a specifically intended response framework.

Figure 5.1 How to Use Trait Bookmarks With Students

Trait Card Bookmarks

Reproduce the bookmarks on the following page, one per student, and mount each on a different colored piece of construction paper, leaving a one- to two-inch border all around the sides. Have each student indicate his or her initials on the back of each bookmark. Laminate for durability.

Teaching and learning practice with bookmarks:

- *Using blank trait bookmarks:* Have students add details to each trait to help them focus on the essence of each trait or use the annotated ones provided.

- *Color-coded traits:* Have the class write and then vote on the best trait color to use for each bookmark. For older students, tie into metaphor discussion. (For the activities below, make sure the whole class uses the same color for each trait.)

- *Trait card collections:* As each trait is introduced, have students make and/or collect cards to use as bookmarks to indicate a section of a shared text or entire book that illustrates the best and/or worst examples of that trait. Follow up with read alouds and class discussion of the reading.

- *Traits up:* For read-aloud participation, begin to read a book or story aloud. Pause and have students hold up the trait they think is best depicted. (With same-color trait cards, the teacher can easily see who is picking which trait.) Have students explain their choices.

- *Jigsaw:* Divide students into equal groups by whichever traits they will be examining. Have that group become that trait's experts and have them discuss the merits of that trait in an indicated piece of writing. Reconfigure the groups so that each new group has one expert for each trait in the group and have them explain their trait group's findings to their new group.

- *Response:* Have students paper-clip a single trait bookmark to a piece of their own writing for peer and/or teacher response, indicating a specific trait for response request.

In dealing with these convergent writing tasks, students need to understand the question and all the subparts it may be asking. In some cases, expected multiple answers are embedded within a single item, for example: "Energy and matter are two factors present in every ecosystem. Explain where most of the energy in an ecosystem originates and how matter is moved through the system." Students must read the test items carefully and plan for responding to all required parts.

Deciding what kind(s) of question the item is asking is an important first step for student writers (see Figure 5.4). Reviewing the interrogative pronouns and their most common usage is helpful for some. When a test item asks students to describe something, it is often asking them to tell *what* something is. For some students, a web or cluster is helpful in organizing

Figure 5.2   Trait Bookmarks

Ideas/Focus

SHOWING, NOT TELLING

DETAILS, DETAILS, DETAILS

Interesting to the reader

Main ideas stand out

Clear and focused

Unusual/small relevant details others might not notice

Design/Organization

Good beginning. Gets your attention.

Transition words

Beginning, middle, end (Plot)

Easy to follow

Sequence makes sense

Satisfying conclusion

Language/Style

"Talking" on paper

Vivid verbs

Words that enliven

Written to be read

Precise nouns

Individuality (your own style)

Sense of audience and purpose

Sentence Fluency/Syntax

SMMMOOOOOOOTH FLOWING

No run-ons or fragments

Rhythm to the piece

Language with a beat

Variety of lengths and structure and beginnings

Standard Conventions

Capitalization   Paragraphs   Grammar and usage

Punctuation correct: periods, commas, quotation marks

Common words spelled correctly

Makes reading simple

Clean copy, publishable, polished work

Figure 5.3   Blank Trait Bookmarks

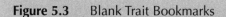

Ideas/Focus

Design/Organization

Language/Style

Sentence Fluency/Syntax

Standard Conventions

Figure 5.4 Deciding What Is Being Asked

Assessment verb	Directions	Nonlinear	Linear
Describe	Tell *what* something is	Web, cluster	List
Contrast	Tell *how* two or more things are contrasted	Venn diagram	T-chart
Cause-effect	Tell *why* two or more things are connected	Tree diagram	Matching lists with arrows
Explain/problem solve	Tell the *how* and *why* of something	Multiple use of above graphic organizers	

information (see Figure 5.5); for others, a list is the easiest means for gathering and organizing their thoughts. When an item asks students *how* two or more things can be compared, the Venn diagram as mentioned in Chapter 2 best meets some students' needs, while a more linear t-chart is preferred by others (see Figure 5.6). Cause-effect items, which ask *why* two or more things are connected, can be brainstormed in a tree diagram; but for others, a graphic with matching lists and arrows is preferred (see Figure 5.7). Those items that ask students to explain a process/concept or solve a problem are often looking for *how* and *why* information and can use a combination of the graphic organizers to best suit students' preferred styles. The important thing for teachers to note is that lots of practice with student thinking and writing about preferred organizers will help students when they are searching for a useful tool during an on-demand writing assessment situation.

Checklists

Interactive writing lessons where the teacher models how to identify the key elements called for in the item is an important first step. Figure 5.8 is a model of a class-developed checklist we have used with students to help them not only begin but also complete the process of responding to a constructed response item. It can be enlarged to poster size and used as a guide for class discussions and reflective writing on the steps that will most likely assist different writers, based on their individual writing and thinking styles.

Figure 5.5   Web for Description

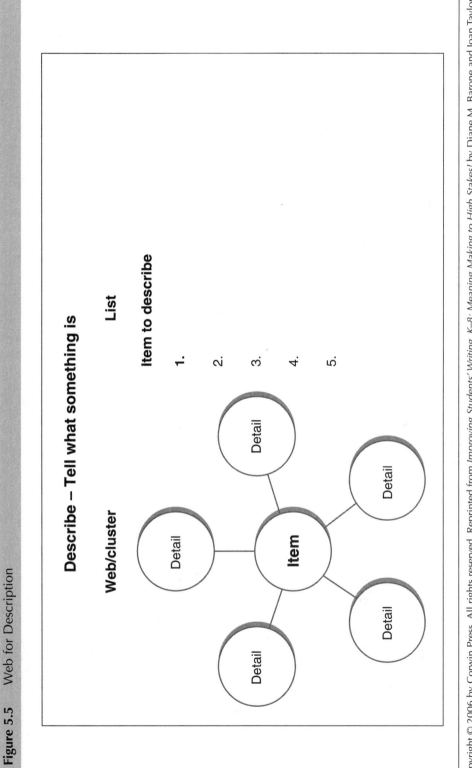

Describe – Tell what something is

Web/cluster   **List**

Item to describe

1.

2.

3.

4.

5.

Figure 5.6   Venn Diagram for Contrast

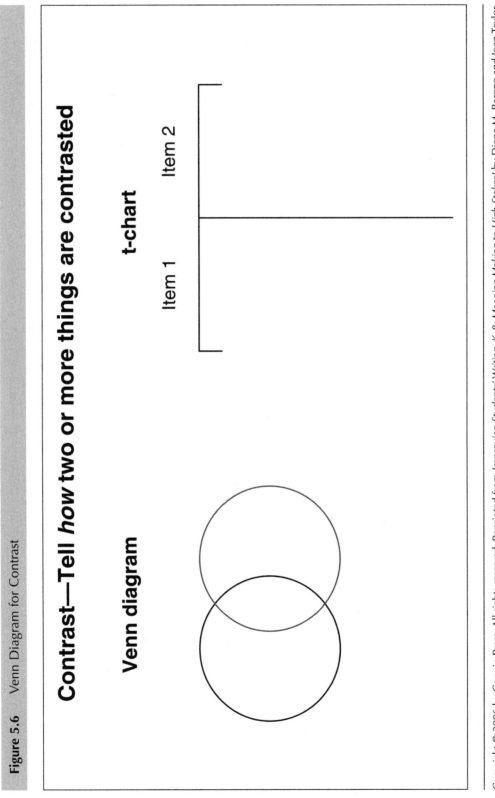

Contrast—Tell *how* two or more things are contrasted

Venn diagram

t-chart

Item 1   Item 2

Figure 5.7 Tree Diagram

Cause/Effect—Tell *why* two or more things are connected

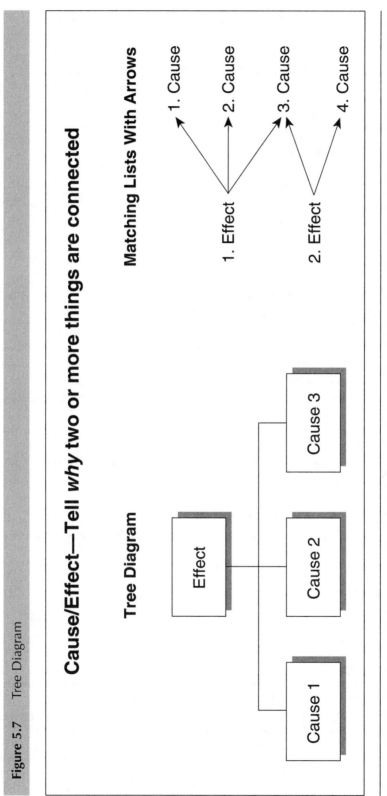

Tree Diagram

Matching Lists With Arrows

Figure 5.8   Classroom-Developed Checklist

Steps for Students in Constructing a Response

Step 1

Because some items have multiple elements embedded in the question, students must read each question carefully and decide all the parts required for a complete response.

Decide what the question is asking for.

Remember that

Who is looking for a person or people.

Where is calling for a place.

When is asking for a date or time.

What is requesting facts.

Why is requiring a reason.

How needs steps.

Explain is asking for information and/or reasons.

Describe is looking for details and/or reasons.

Step 2

Turn the question into a topic sentence answer.

Example: What will Goldilocks do the next time she wanders into a vacant house?

Response: The next time Goldilocks wanders across a vacant house, she will probably . . .

Step 3

Collect needed information.

Go back to the passage and list, cluster, draw, or in some way gather the reasons for your answer. Make sure you get all the relevant details you will need.

Step 4

Organize the reasons in a logical order.

Show your reader where you have included details from the passage or how you have solved the problem.

Step 5

Write your answer.

Make sure your writing is legible so that readers will be able to understand what you are saying.

Step 6

Reread and check your answer.

Review the question and your answer, **making sure you completely answered all parts of the question** and that your details and information are accurate.

Repeat Steps 5 and 6 until you are satisfied with your response. Sometimes you can go back and check other test items and then come back to this one for a final check.

Self-check lists are also helpful in ensuring complete responses to convergent items. Editing lists, particularly those adapted to individual student needs and those that separate tasks such as capitalization, punctuation, paragraphing, spelling, usage, and sentence structure into more manageable steps, are helpful to students. Student participation in the development of these checklists is crucial to their successful implementation.

Rubrics

Rubrics can also be generated and used as part of an interactive writing model. From a generic framework, as shown in Figure 5.9, a more precisely worded rubric can be constructed as a means of looking for all the parts of a complete response in other content areas. For example, the general rubric in Figure 5.9 can be revised as part of a whole class discussion for a reading, math, or science question, as shown in Figures 5.10, 5.11, and 5.12.

Then students may work individually to respond to the items and discuss their responses in a group to help them revise their individual pieces to incorporate all the needed information. As a class, they can share group responses to facilitate discussion on how their responses might be scored, and then they can revise their own pieces to practice completing comprehensive responses to the items.

After several sessions of this type of practice, the class can write sample papers for each of the scores designed for another task. By purposely developing low- to high-quality levels of responses, students can see the variations and pitfalls of the constructed response item format. Later, using the provided rubrics, they can also practice responding to these questions on their own, and then, using the rubric as a checklist, they can self-assess their efforts as the first reader and/or scorer of their piece of writing.

PRODUCT VERSUS PROCESS

The current focus on writing assessment has at times redirected our efforts from writing as a process to writing for a product. Maintaining a balance between the two is a challenge for writing teachers everywhere. Excellent teachers are finding ways to blend the two so students continue to be engaged in writing as an activity for learning as well as for demonstrating proficiency.

(Text Continued on page 120)

Figure 5.9   Generic Framework for a Rubric

General Scoring Rubric for Convergent Writing Tasks

Score Point	Expectation
3	The response completely and accurately answers all parts of the item and displays thorough understanding of the standard(s) and/or skill(s) within the standard being assessed. It displays all or most of the following: • Provides sufficient, relevant details that clearly indicate the ideas and processes used to support the answer. • When required, provides problem-solving techniques, evidence, and labeling to support the response.
2	The response partially but adequately answers the question and displays satisfactory understanding of the standard(s) and/or skill(s) being assessed. It exhibits all or most of the following: • Provides adequate details that indicate that ideas and processes are understood, but is somewhat limited or general. • Adequately completes all or part of the task, but may demonstrate minor errors in the answer and/or reasoning.
1	The response demonstrates a vague or limited understanding of the standard(s) and/or skill(s) being tested. It is flawed in some or all of the following ways: • Contains unrelated details or fails to provide details that indicate ideas and processes are completely understood; response may reveal a misunderstanding of what is being asked in the item. • Inadequately completes essential parts of the task and/or contains flaws in demonstrating support and reasoning.
0	The response is extremely weak and fails to indicate an understanding of the standard(s) and/or skill(s) being tested. It illustrates some or all of the following: • Gives an answer that is unrelated to the item or is incorrect based on information provided. • Repeats the item but adds nothing to show understanding of the task being measured.

Figure 5.10 Rubric for a Reading Task and Sample Responses

Specific Scoring Rubric for Reading Task

Sample item:

In the story, Hansel and Gretel stop at the gingerbread house to find their way home. Using information from the passage, explain why they might not stop at a gingerbread house if they become lost in the woods again.

Score Point	Expectation
3	The response completely explains why Hansel and Gretel might not stop at a gingerbread house in the future. The response includes sufficient, relevant supporting details from the passage.
2	The response explains why Hansel and Gretel might not stop at a gingerbread house in the future. The response includes some relevant details from the passage but may contain a few inaccuracies or minimal details.
1	Response attempts to explain why Hansel and Gretel might not stop at a gingerbread house in the future. The response may contain numerous inaccuracies or misunderstandings about the passage. Few, if any, relevant details from the passage are provided.
0	The response is totally inaccurate and/or irrelevant.

Sample Responses to Reading Rubric

3 – In the future, Hansel and Gretel might not stop at a gingerbread house and ask for directions because while the old woman seemed friendly, she was really a wicked witch who tried to harm them. In the story, she locked Hansel up and planned to kill him and she made Gretel do lots of hard work. They escaped, but probably learned a lesson and would be very careful before going into a place like that again.

2 – Hansel and Gretel might not stop at a gingerbread house in the future because the house may look different. It looked inviting the first time, but the witch was really bad.

1 – Hansel and Gretel might not stop at the gingerbread house in the future because the witch was magic. She put a spell on them and they were afraid. They will look for another place next time.

0 – The house was down. The witch lived happily ever after.

Figure 5.11 Rubric for a Math Task and Sample Responses

Specific Scoring Rubric for Math Task

Sample item:

A. What is the mode, median, and mean for each of the following class's scores?

Mrs. Baldwin's class: 80, 57, 52, 68, 34, 73, 52, 64, 69

Mr. Green's class: 48, 43, 52, 78, 51, 84, 78

Show your work and explain how you obtained your answers.

Score Point	Expectation
3	The response gives the correct answers for all parts of the problem and completely demonstrates and explains how each answer was derived.
2	The response gives correct answers for most of the parts of the problem and explains how the answer was derived OR the response gives correct answers to all parts but provides incomplete information on how answers were derived OR the response indicates understanding and explanation of all parts but contains some significant computational errors.
1	The response may supply some correct answers but not provide clearly acceptable answers for most parts of the problem OR response gives correct answers to all parts but omits all information on how answers were derived OR supplies some correct answers but indicates minimal understanding of the problem and contains numerous computational errors.
0	The response is totally inaccurate and/or irrelevant.

Sample Responses to Math Rubric

3

Baldwin's class	Green's class
80	
57	
52	48
68	43
34	52
73	78
52	51

64 + 69 549	84 + 78 434
549/9 = 61 is the mean I added up all the numbers and divided by the number of tests.	434/7 = 62 is the mean I added up all the numbers and divided by the number of tests.
The mode is 52 because it is the score that occurs the most.	The mode is 78 because it is the score that occurs the most.
34, 52, 57, 64, 68, 69, 73, 80 The median is 68 because it is the middle point of the numbers when they are arranged from smallest to largest.	43, 48, 51, 52, 78, 78, 84 The median is 52 because it is the middle point of the numbers when they are arranged from smallest to largest.

Sample Responses to Math Rubric

2

Baldwin's class	Green's class
80 57 52 68 34 73 52 64 + 69 549	48 43 52 78 51 84 + 78 434
549/9 = 61 is the mean	434/7 = 62 is the mean
The mode is 80.	The mode is 84.
34, 52, 57, 64, 68, 69, 73, 80 The median is 68 because it is the middle point of the numbers.	43, 48, 51, 52, 78, 78, 84 The median is 52 because it is the middle point of the numbers.

(Continued)

Sample Responses to Math Rubric

1

Baldwin's class	Green's class
80 57 52 68 34 73 52 64 + 69 ——— 549	48 43 52 78 51 84 + 78 ——— 434
The mean is 61.	The mean is 62.
The mode is 80.	The mode is 84.
The median is 61.	The median is 62.

0

Baldwin's class	Green's class
The mean is 80, 57, 52, 68, 34, 73, 52, 64, 69.	The mean is 48, 43, 52, 78, 51, 84, 78
The mode is.	The mode is over the top.
The median is the line	The median is

Practice in writing to divergent and convergent writing prompts should model some of the important lessons learned over the past 30 years of process writing reform. Both types of writing purposes follow the familiar, recursive writing activities that overlap interconnect prewriting, writing, and revision. Teachers can provide prewriting opportunities and organizers for generating initial responses. They can also model mini-lesson writing techniques (Atwell, 1987) and then allow sufficient practice time to imitate and experiment with some of the ideas presented. Perhaps most important is the need to offer safe, non-evaluative opportunities to share with other writers and to reflect and revise and celebrate the application of new techniques.

Figure 5.12 Rubric for a Science Task and Sample Responses

Specific Scoring Rubric for Science

Sample item:

Explain how plucking the strings of the guitar will make a sound.

Give at least two ways the sound can be made to produce a lower pitch and a higher pitch.

Show your work and explain how you obtained your answers.

Score Point	Expectation
3	The response completely answers all parts of the test item through displaying knowledge of basic facts, conceptual understanding, and/ or practical reasoning of the standard being tested. The response provides an answer that clearly and correctly • Indicates the scientific ideas applied and provides evidence of understanding • Labels all answers, if required
2	The response gives correct answers for most parts of the test item and displays satisfactory knowledge of basic facts, conceptual understanding, and/or practical reasoning of the science standard being assessed. The response provides an answer that • Correctly completes all parts of the task but may contain minor flaws or incomplete/incorrect portions • Completes the entire task but uses some incomplete, or partially complete information
1	The response demonstrates a limited understanding of the knowledge of basic facts, conceptual understanding, and/or practical reasoning of the science standard being assessed. The response provides an answer that • May contain significant errors and/or misconceptions in the response • Offers an acceptable response for one part, but fails to attempt a solution to the other part(s)
0	The response demonstrates a lack of understanding of basic facts, conceptual understanding, and/or practical reasoning of the science standard being tested. The response provides an answer that • Contains insufficient evidence of appropriate skills and/or knowledge • Provides incorrect or inappropriate responses to the question, OR • There is no response

Sample Responses to Science Rubric

3

The strings vibrate as they are plucked and produce sounds. The strings could be pulled tighter to produce a higher sound and could be made looser to produce a lower sound. If thicker strings were substituted the sound would be lower; if thinner strings were used the sound would be higher.

2

The vibration of the strings causes the sounds. The strings could be shortened to make a higher pitch. The strings could be plucked harder to make a lower sound.

1

Plucking the strings makes a sound. It will be lower if the strings are not pulled tight. It will be softer if the strings are plucked softly.

0

I like to play the guitar because it is fun and I can make music.

Practicing in a variety of modes and for different audiences and purposes are important procedures for all writing instruction. One advantage of the rubric model of writing assessments is that it provides the writer with a window into the readers' thinking and judgment criteria. Teachers, in writing with their students, can discuss how they might deal with some of the practice items in preparation for the assessment with a known audience. Students like Todd, described earlier in Miss Farley's class, might then better understand exactly what is expected of them in terms of proficient writing and revising. In addition, as teachers read aloud for and with students on a regular basis, they can examine and discuss how and why certain writing styles might be viewed differently by various audiences.

Writing pieces focused on the assessment genre, like self-selected writing topics, do not need to go though the entire writing process, though a number should eventually be shared with writing groups and become published. It is important to structure opportunities for students to self-evaluate their assessment writing in personal reflections, teacher-student conferences, and in peer review situations.

FINAL THOUGHTS

The purposes of assessing student writing are varied. If the intent is formative response and feedback, response activities as described in Chapter 4 are most appropriate. However, for accountability testing information, holistic systems are most often used to provide numerical scores for reporting purposes. Most reporting agencies use either focused holistic or analytic trait scoring methods. Both have their strengths and weaknesses. Writing scholars (Cooper, 1997; Mayher, 1990; National Council of Teachers of English, 1995; White, 1994) urge the use of writing assessments that provide easily understandable criteria for students, teachers, parents, and administrators or policymakers and these two methods seem best able to provide those conditions.

One of the most vocal criticisms of focused holistic measures points out that when evaluators rate writing pieces holistically, based on general merit, their reasoning may appear vague and does not indicate exactly what is valued. They may favor certain personally significant qualities that bias their opinion of the whole composition. However, according to Applebee (1994), one of the advantages of holistic scoring is its tendency to *level* topic differences.

On the other hand, critics of analytic trait scoring note the separation of a whole piece of writing into discrete parts. They point out that separating and analyzing discrete writing traits is a little like making and eating parts of a meal. While you can certainly predict the quality of the meal by its individual dishes, sometimes they just don't all fit well together. However, its use as a direct link to specific diagnostic information is valuable.

Computer programs designed to provide evaluative information on student writing, which are sometimes merely elaborate versions of spelling and/or grammar checks that are standard features on most word processing programs, are becoming increasingly more sophisticated in their abilities to provide immediate feedback to student writers. Their ease of use and speed in reporting are attractive attributes for administrators and policymakers.

Assessment writing has become its own genre in terms of importance to teachers and students, often using traditional, rote-style, formulaic approaches to instruction (Hillocks, 2002). With the advent of the current accountability climate in which we live, students are being asked to demonstrate writing proficiency in both convergent, narrowly focused tasks, and divergent, broadly based tasks, sometimes in a variety of genres in a test-taking setting. A single piece of writing can sometimes be the crucial and often single criterion used in some high-stakes accountability writing tests today, even for students as young as eight years of age. This places a burden of stress on teachers of writing who view writing as a means of expressing and constructing thinking.

The test-taking mode of writing as an additional, though not all-important, genre must be relegated to its proper place of importance in the writing curriculum, that is, one part of the multiple genres and reasons for writing. The research-based methods of teaching writing must become incorporated into best practices and writing programs instead of being preempted by quick-fix approaches. With such an emphasis on assessments, teachers must find balance between purposes and genres, as well as correction and encouragement, so that students progress in their writing proficiency, not just as test takers, but also as thinkers and communicators and as lifelong readers and writers.

6 Connecting Writing and Classroom Conversation

Mrs. Caitlen, a sixth-grade teacher, requests that her students write in their math journal, "What does equivalent mean? Is 2/3 equivalent to 6/10? Why or why not?" Anthony walks up to Jana and says, "I am not sure what I should do." Mrs. Caitlen replies to Anthony, "Think about our math work yesterday and see if you can remember anything having to do with equivalency." Anthony goes back to his desk and starts manipulating the fractions of 2/3 and 6/10. He slowly starts to write in his journal. He often stops and checks out what other students are doing, looks at the teacher, and goes back to his writing. When Jana observes that students have stopped writing, she asks, "Can you explain equivalency?" Michael answers, "No, they are not equivalent. I think equivalent means equal." Lisa replies, "I am not sure. I couldn't figure out how to reduce 6/10 to see if it is the same as 2/3." Anthony enters into the conversation: "I thought this was hard too. I divided 2 into the 6 and the 10 and got 3/5 and then I knew they weren't the same. So I think equivalency must have to do with whether they are the same or not." "I am pleased to learn how you solved this problem. You have been using what we learned before to help you here. That is what mathematicians do. So now how about if we look at how you find the lowest terms," Mrs. Caitlen commented.

I n this simple conversation, Mrs. Caitlen allowed her students to think through writing about the mathematics term *equivalency* and provided a problem to help with this thinking. Once students committed to what equivalency was and decided if the fractions were equivalent, she engaged them in discussion. Mrs. Caitlen was very careful how she responded to her students in that she acknowledged their thinking and suggested they were thinking like mathematicians. She did not chastise them by saying that they should have easily understood this information, as they had worked on it for several days. Her goal was to support her students, encourage their thinking, and help them make this knowledge their own.

ACADEMIC CONVERSATIONS

In this chapter we explore informal and formal, oral and written academic conversations that can support or stifle student learning. The words that teachers choose to respond to student work are important to student learning (Johnston, 2004). They can result in exploration and further learning by students, as seen in the above example, or they can shut them down or lead to false starts.

Informal Oral and Written Conversations

Informal oral conversations often occur *on the run* as students ask a question and expect an immediate answer from a teacher. These conversations can be about academics or they might be personal in nature, where a student is sharing an important event with his or her teacher. Informal written conversations generally occur as a teacher writes back to a student about a journal entry. These journals might be general, focused on content, or in particular on reading. For informal conversations, teachers' responses are directed to the content of the message, not on conventions.

These conversations either orally or in writing are critical in building relationships with students and in helping students develop their competence and identity as readers and writers. Johnston (2004) documents the importance of language in explaining students' success at becoming literate. He argues that it is "the subtle ways in which they [teachers] build emotionally and relationally healthy learning communities—intellectual environments that produce not mere technical competence, but caring, secure, actively literate human beings" (p. 2). He goes on to explain the critical role of teachers in responding to students' comments. He writes, "Talk is the central tool of their trade. With it they mediate children's activity and experience, and help them make sense of learning, literacy, life, and themselves" (p. 4).

The following examples from oral classroom conversations and journal entries demonstrate how teachers further student learning. This discursive learning pushes students beyond their current understanding of content knowledge and the writing process.

Our first example comes from the classroom of Vivian Paley (1981). Paley was a kindergarten teacher who wrote about the extensive conversations that occurred in her classroom. What is interesting about these conversations is that she provided a thought-provoking question and then she expected her students to contemplate it and respond to one another. Following is one of these conversations focused on language:

Teacher: If you were in charge of the world, would you make only one language or many languages?

Tanya: One language, oh yes! Then I could understand everyone in the whole world.

Eddie: No, let it stay this way so different countries keep on being not the same. Then you take trips to see what those countries are like and how they talk.

Teacher: Is that because they have different languages?

Ellen: I like the world the way it is but I don't like the fighting.

Wally: She means like if someone says, "Let's play," in French, then in Chinese they might think he said, "Let's fight."

Warren: Keep it this way because if you're Chinese you would have to learn English. (p. 119)

This conversation continues as the children problematize the issue of language. This simple conversation in kindergarten allows students to recognize that their ideas are valid and not similar. They listen to one another and build from what was said, as is demonstrated in the interactions between Tanya and Eddie and Wally and Warren. Paley carefully nudged students' thinking with the questions she posed. Her questions did not have clear answers, and students had to search for possible solutions, as is demonstrated in their pondering of one or more languages for the world. Paley used these conversations as frames for stories that children created and acted out. Through this process, students understood how ideas were explored socially and how they could be organized into oral stories that they performed for classmates. It is easy to hypothesize how these oral conversations and stories will positively serve children when they begin to write their own.

In the next example, Anthony meets his sixth-grade teacher for a conversation about a story he is writing. Anthony shows his teacher some of the revising and editing he is currently working on.

Teacher: How are you today, Anthony?

Anthony: Fine. I am working on my paper. I wanted to show you some changes I made to see what you think. I'm having a hard time with this one part.

Teacher: I see you are using this opportunity to make your paper better. Most people need to revise and edit their work. Remember, you helped me with the changes to my story. I kept getting the part confused about the kids doing their work. I'm glad you are not just leaving mistakes and confusions in your writing. You know most authors have editors who help them get their writing better.

The conversation continues as Anthony and his teacher check out a particularly troubling part of Anthony's writing.

This short conversation accomplishes many positive things to help Anthony and other students in this room develop as writers. First off, the teacher shares that he is a writer and he has had to revise his work to get it right. Here Anthony and his teacher are colleagues who share similar difficulties with writing, and they provide help to one another. Second, Anthony learns that all writers, even accomplished ones, depend on editors to improve their writing. And finally, Anthony and his teacher engage in conversation about writing where both contribute to making his writing more comprehensible.

Most important, in this example the teacher did not take control of Anthony's writing. Even though he is a more experienced writer than Anthony, they worked together to get a solution that was pleasing to Anthony. This kind of support is not always easy for teachers to give. Often, because we as teachers can see easy ways to clear up miscommunications in writing, we want to quickly offer solutions. Anthony's teacher was able to forgo the quick solution and work with Anthony so that in the future, Anthony will be a more capable writer.

This brief encounter could have stifled Anthony's writing if his teacher had not responded to Anthony's writing needs. Perhaps when Anthony approached his teacher, the teacher might have said, "Sorry, Anthony, you need to work alone right now." This response would have sent Anthony to his desk where he might or might not have worked on his writing. As is evident in the above conversation, Anthony needed a more experienced colleague to help him over a writing hurdle. Being sent to work alone would most likely not have resolved his current writing dilemma.

The next example comes from a series of journal entries that Eric wrote to his teacher. His teacher used journals to help her understand her students and their in-school and out-of-school strengths and interests. In responding to "What do you like about yourself," Eric wrote:

> I like that I am a good soccer player and a better tetherball player. I like that I am good at long division and studying. I also like that I am a good friend and a good big brother to my sister and my brothers. One thing I like about myself is I can listen and concentrate when I'm doing homework or studying. [no corrections]

Teacher's reply:

> Eric, I am so pleased to know that you like to play soccer and tetherball. Are you going to try out for our school soccer team? I think you might like playing. And I can tell that you must be a good student. I am impressed that in sixth grade you know how to study and that you do all your homework. Tell me about a book that you enjoy reading at home. Maybe we have the same interests. I watched you help your brother when he visited our room. You are a good brother. Are your little brothers and sister fun to play with?

Eric shared many important details about himself as a person in his entry. He understands much about himself already: he is an athlete, a good student, and a good big brother. His teacher acknowledged his strengths and nudged him to extend them, as seen in her suggestion to join the soccer team. And like the conversation between Anthony and his teacher, she encouraged Eric to volunteer a favorite book so that they could share conversations about books. Her personal written response to Eric showed him that his teacher valued him as a learner and as a person, important knowledge in supporting student learners (Benard, 2004).

While the messages carried in the above written conversations are the most important element, Eric's teacher is also supporting his reading and writing development. Eric learned that he can carry on a personal conversation with his teacher. The richer and more complete his message is, the more substantial the response is from his teacher. He learned that writing is a valuable mode of communication, and in this case it allowed him to develop a personal relationship with his teacher.

Eric's teacher took the necessary time to carefully respond to Eric, but what if she had just responded "Good work" or nothing at all. Then this opportunity to learn about Eric and support him as a learner would have been lost. Most likely, Eric's journal contributions would be shorter in the future and not particularly meaningful. Eric might continue to write to explore ideas for himself or to fulfill the expectation for journal writing, but he would not have the opportunity to participate in rich conversations with his teacher about himself and his learning.

In the final example, a student carried on an academic conversation centered on reading with her teacher. Following are several journal entries that were written when Alison and a group of students, including her teacher, were reading *From the Mixed-up Files of Mrs. Basil E. Frankweiler* (Konigsburg, 1967). In this book a brother and sister run away to the Metropolitan Museum of Art. They live there for two weeks and try to discover if a statue was created by Michelangelo. Alison wrote:

> Claudia didn't regret bringing Jamie along because he had a transistor radio. She appointed him treasurer and he had to keep track of all the money. He tried to get her to change her mind and go to Central Park but she said they might get mugged or robbed or kidnapped. [no corrections]

Teacher's response:

> He did have things she might need like the radio and he was good with money. I think the museum is a better place than Central Park. I think it might be safer with the guards there.

Alison's entry:

> I didn't quite understand when Claudia knelt beside Jamie and they prayed and Claudia said "C'mon let's go to the statue." Who's C'mon? [no corrections]

Teacher's response:

> I went and reread that part. I can see how it was confusing. *C'mon* is not a person. It just is short for "come on." Why don't you go back and reread that part and see if it makes more sense. Let me know what happens.

Alison's entry:

> I read, "This ain't no highway." It sounds like they are Valley. Valley means they talk like gag me with a fork dude and they're saying ain't. And ain't doesn't mean anything. Then he said, "I tell ya, this dame's loaded." I think dame's means car or bus or truck because they said it is loaded but it could mean something else like suitcase. [corrected spelling]

Teacher's response:

> I can see where you think this sounds like Valley language. The taxi driver doesn't talk the way Claudia does. He has an interesting dialect. I like the way you tried to figure out the word *dame's*. You came up with two great possible meanings for this word. There is at least one more and that one is that *dame* is a lady.

Alison continued to correspond in writing with her teacher throughout the book. She also had conversations with the other students reading this book. Alison's teacher supported her meaning making when she helped her decide who *C'mon* was or wasn't and in her trying to figure out the meaning of *dame's*. She also extended her knowledge by offering the word *dialect* to explain the taxi driver's interesting speech.

Alison, like Eric, learned to communicate about her reading and learning through writing. She understood that writing clarified her thinking about her reading and offered a way to share her thoughts with another interested reader. And her teacher had a vehicle to clarify and extend Allison's understandings and also to learn about what hindered Alison's reading comprehension. For example, most teachers would not have anticipated that the contraction *c'mon* would present such confusion.

As was shared with the other examples, the conversations shared orally and in writing are what is important to student learning. In each example, teachers found the time to listen carefully to individual students and then to respond in consequential ways to their thoughts. Through this personal response, teachers built relationships with students and clarified or extended their content knowledge. They also modeled and extended students' ability to think through writing and to communicate effectively through writing.

Teachers' comments can nudge students' identities so that they see themselves as literate individuals. The conversational examples positioned students to be active agents in their learning. Dyson (1999) wrote, "A child must have some version of, 'Yes, I imagine I can do this.' And a teacher must also view the present child as competent and on that basis imagine new possibilities" (pp. 396–397). Certainly, Anthony's, Eric's, and Alison's teachers saw that their students were competent. They treated them as colleagues as they worked together on writing or through writing.

Johnston (2004) offers phrases that teachers might use to support students' active engagement with their own learning. For example, teachers might ponder the following:

- What are you doing as a writer today?
- What have you learned as a writer?
- What problems did you encounter in your writing? How did you solve them?
- Where do you see this writing going? Will it become a persuasive piece?

Johnston (2004) argues that agency in students matters. Children who are passive in their approaches to learning doubt their competence and set low goals that are easy to attain. If they face difficulty, they become disengaged and lose concentration. However, "Children with strong belief in their own agency work harder, focus their attention better, are more interested in their studies, and are less likely to give up when they encounter difficulties" (pp. 40–41).

As shown in the above examples, teachers can support students in becoming and developing the belief that they are capable as learners, even when they encounter difficulties. Anthony's teacher validated that Anthony is a writer, like professional writers, who would benefit from the help of an editor. Eric's teacher learned through Eric's writing that Eric saw himself competent in many areas, but especially in learning, for he

Figure 6.1 Page From Sherry's Book

this strategy, she focused on only one vignette, and then successive parts provided additional events. Nicole used this strategy to scaffold additional stories where she continued with the same characters. This allowed her to share published stories with the class on numerous occasions, rather than waiting to share only one story with numerous parts. Following is her story without revision or corrections.

The small ist dog

Prt one

The small ist. dog he had no fren's. he was vre sad. Im glad im not him. I fell sre for him. And he is a brown dog wite three blak spos. he sooe a big mean dog. he was sowe big like a bear. he loke at him in a mean look. He was all blak. Thae met a bear. and thae all mad fren's evne the sadog mad fans with the big dog. The small dog is happy now.

Nicole brought her story to her teacher at the end of writing workshop. Her teacher decided to write to Nicole about her story and to suggest she have a conference with her the next day. This is what her teacher wrote:

I can tell that your story is about a sad dog who has no friends. I am guessing that he is sad because he wants friends. Am I right? I like all the details you gave me about the dog like his colors and that he has only three black spots. He must be very cute. And I like how you compared the one dog to a bear. I can see how big he is. It was interesting to hear about the mean dog. I don't know if I would feel safe getting near him. The sad dog was brave.

I think we should have a chat about your story tomorrow. Help me understand why the mean dog was mean and how they saw a bear. I am a little bit confused about that part.

During writing workshop on the following day, Nicole and her teacher shared reading Nicole's story. They both read together so that Nicole could listen as her teacher read it more fluently. Following is part of a conversation that Nicole had with her teacher about this story:

Nicole: I like writing about the sad dog and I think I might have three parts.

Teacher: So you will keep sharing more about the sad dog. Will the mean dog and the bear be part of the story?

Nicole: I think so. I am thinking of Morris and Boris and how they are friends in the book and I want my story like that.

Teacher: Okay, I understand. So you are writing a book about friends.

Nicole: Yes.

Teacher: As I listen to this story, I am wondering why the dog is sad and the other is mean. Can you help me figure that out?

The conversation continues as Nicole provides reasons for the dogs' emotions. Later she works at incorporating this background into her story. For Part 1 of her story, these were the only revisions that happened. It would take until Part 2 to find out how the dogs became friends with a bear.

In this example, Nicole's teacher had to be patient. Nicole had taken on the task of writing multiple short stories that would be grouped to form a larger text, as she had seen in Wiseman's Morris and Boris books she was reading. Her teacher decided to help Nicole with providing support for the emotions of the dogs she wrote about. While she might have chosen the development of friendships, she chose a simpler task for Nicole's revision. Later, as Nicole's drafts provided evidence of characters' feelings, she will nudge Nicole to add details about relationship building. There will be many opportunities to do so in forthcoming parts to this story. Nicole's teacher will gradually build Nicole's writing skills. For now, she is pleased that Nicole is trying to replicate the kind of story written by professional authors and is extending her current knowledge and competence as a writer.

In the next example, Bryan, a third grader, wrote a story called *The Naughty Kids*. His teacher was worried about the violence that kept showing up in Bryan's writing. While she had talked to him about not including so much violence, Bryan continued. She decided to have the students in the class, first, second, and third graders, respond to his writing. Because Bryan was a leader in the class, students listened to him read his story, and then they wrote responses to him that they could sign or not sign. Their teacher chose writing primarily so that students could continue being Bryan's friend even if they wrote critical responses, and she wanted them to move to written response so their comments might be more thoughtful.

Following is Bryan's story as he read it without revision or final editing.

The Naughty Kids

Once upon a time there were naughty naughty kids. They would brake windows and brake lamps and pop tires take chains off bikes and take bolts out of bikes. So the wheels would fall off and so peple would brake there arms when they fell off.

> At home the two kids where so mean to there sisters and there little brother and they nevere got in troubl and they got away with everything they did.
>
> At school they would beat up on kids. School was the best place to be naughty to the teachers and the prinsubul. Finaly the teachers called the to naughty kids' mom and dad. The kids names are Bryan and Chris.
>
> So there mom and did not care about that. The next day the kids played muchen guns and guns and they where waring camouflage pants.
>
> The naughty kids desided that they where being selfish and so they stop being naughty.

After Bryan read his story, students quietly wrote comments. There was great variety in responses, although most students focused in on the violence. Following are several responses:

Amanda: I liked your story. Chris and you sound mischievous.

Aaron: I don't think you should have all that violence in your story. Did you do anything that wasn't violent?

Heather: Show what you guys did besides beating up kids.

Chakela: I like your story, but can't you tell something besides beating up kids, even though you might have beat them up.

Bryan brought these comments to the teacher and they read them together. After listening, Bryan said, "I thought they would think it was funny. Chris and I were pretty bad. I guess I need to add something else, like when we did get in trouble for what we did." His teacher decided to let Bryan revise his work without further comment from her. He continued to work on this story for several days, and then he abandoned it for another. When his teacher asked about it, he said, "I am not interested anymore. It was too hard to change."

This example demonstrates a method that a teacher used to diffuse a student who continued to write violent stories. Perhaps she could have been more direct in her comments to him, but as his story said, "School was the best place to be naughty." She did not want to get into a power struggle with Bryan about the content of his writing and shut him off from writing for the classroom audience. Instead, she asked students to respond, and their responses nudged Bryan to move to other topics for writing.

Moving from narrative writing for a moment, the next example is an informational piece written by a fourth-grade student, Ryan. Ryan enjoyed writing about animals. Most of his writing throughout the year was focused on various animals. At first he wrote a few paragraphs on an animal, and his teacher nudged him to write longer pieces. Here is his first-draft writing about whales as he wrote it:

Whales

The blue whale is the biggest animal that ever lived. They normally live in the Antarctic.

The killer whale has a very good name because he goes around killing other whales. The killer whale has a very big mouth and very sharp teeth.

Whales have very smol hairs on them.

Some whales have beak type things like the dolphin.

If you think the whale is an anfibean you are wrong. A whale is not an anfibean. Whales live in different places.

The gray whale is very big but it is not the biggest thing that ever lived.

The clown whale will swim around with groups and go up and down and sing sort of like a song.

Ryan brought this piece of writing to his teacher and asked, "I like writing about whales. I know a lot about them. I am not sure how to end this."

Similar to other teachers, she asked Ryan to read his writing to her. Following is part of their conversation after he read:

Teacher: Ryan, you do have a lot of information. How did you find it all?

Ryan: I got books in the library and I looked on the Internet.

Teacher: So how did you know what to use?

Ryan: I picked from both. That is where I learned about all the kinds of whales.

Teacher: So, Ryan, I know you want help with ending this writing. Can you help me know what you wanted us to learn from this?

Ryan: I want everyone to get excited about whales. And I want them to know about them.

Teacher: I think they will get excited when they learn about them. I am thinking that if that is what you want to do, you might start your writing with some information about all whales. See here where you wrote . . .

Learning what was important to Ryan about this writing guided the teacher in how she responded. Before she could give an answer on how he might finish his writing, she learned about Ryan's goal. Because Ryan wanted to share information that students would be excited about, she helped him with his structure first. This was a slight detour from Ryan's primary goal; however, this rewriting focused Ryan on sharing information. Once this reorganization occurred, she helped him provide additional details about whales and what they were if they were not amphibians. She also complimented him on his voice that was so dominant when he asked his readers questions about whales. Ryan decided to incorporate this structure in his writing when he provided information about whales. He wrote:

> Did you know there is a whale called a killer whale? Well there is and this is why he got that name.

He used this format for each whale. He also came up with an ending that shared his enthusiasm for whales. He wrote:

> I shared some information about whales, but there is lots more to learn. If you go to www.enchantedlearning.com, you can learn more. Then maybe we can work on a book together.

This ending matches the voice he used throughout his writing as he brought readers in through his questions. He ends by opening up the possibility of working together to expand knowledge about whales in succeeding books.

The next two examples come from the sixth grade. Teachers were very busy preparing students for the state writing assessment. Unlike the earlier examples, these teachers spoke to the whole class on writing, and all students were expected to write an essay on a singular topic. Below is some of what was said by one teacher before they worked on a sample prompt—"An accomplishment I am proud of."

Teacher: What are you going to do with the word *accomplishment*? You have to refer to the prompt in the first sentence.

Student: The time when I made someone feel happy.

Student: The time that I made an accomplishment that I am proud of.

Student: My accomplishment was about my favorite things.

Teacher: You might want to change this to my most outstanding accomplishment. The judges want to know your biggest accomplishment. They want you to tell them in your writing.

Student: The accomplishment that changed my life.

Teacher: You nailed it. You addressed the prompt and you used key words. I love this one.

Teacher: I think the prewriting helps. Use it to get your ideas down. Use strong verbs in each sentence. It is important to use strong, lively verbs in writing and descriptive adjectives. You will get big points for those. Use metaphors and similes. I know you remember what they are. Now start writing.

Once these directions were provided, students quietly wrote about an accomplishment. A few wrote notes, but most just began writing. In this brief conversation by the teacher, it was clear that she wanted them to think of many aspects of writing simultaneously for this test. They had to write a strong introduction that included key words from the prompt. They were to provide details and use strong verbs, adjectives, metaphors, and similes. Following is one example of the resultant writing.

I was proud when I got better grades than I had. I used to be sad because my brother got better grades then me when he was in second grade. My parents told me that I shouldn't believe my brother because you're smart and if you believe in yourself you will get good grades too, but I still felt sad.

When I went to 5th grade I had Mr. Martin he was trying to make me believe in myself more and more he always said to me, "Don't give up and keep on trying." I was trying so hard because he made the day fun. My first report card came as and A's and B's. So by the end of the year I got a certificate I was so happy. My mom and dad were so

> happy to. I will always thank Mr. Martin for the help he gave me. My brother can't call me dumb anymore.
>
> Now I am thinking why was I believing my brother when I could always get good grades. If I just believed in myself. Now my friends Vanessa and Josie are cheering me on but I don't need it anymore. I feel good of myself and I believe in myself. Now I know knowbody gets the same grades. If you try you will do it!!! My accomplishment can make a big difference in life. [no corrections]

Brooke's writing is interesting, particularly after listening to her teacher's directions. Brooke started out with her dilemma of not being particularly successful in school and her brother's harassment. Her essay moves to how a teacher made a difference to her and helped her achieve her accomplishment of being a successful student. Finally, in the last sentence she mentions the word *accomplishment*. For Brooke, the message of her essay was her focus on academic achievement, and this is evident in the strength of her voice. Unfortunately, when Brooke's teacher wrote comments to her, she did not highlight this aspect of her writing. She wrote:

> I want you to use key words in your first sentence. I did not see strong verbs or metaphors. You need to include them.

Perhaps because the writing test was a stressful, high-stakes event, her teacher focused on small elements of this writing, rather than the message conveyed and how that might be improved.

In the next example, a sixth-grade teacher also helped students prepare for the state writing test. For this writing the prompt was "How I would change the world." Following is the conversation he had with students before they began to write to this prompt:

Teacher: We get to practice for the writing test again. I have noticed how you have used notes to organize your thinking. I think when I read your essays this has helped you get the big ideas down. So I want you to continue doing this. Today as you plan your writing, think of some interesting words you might use for words you always use. Can you think of a word you like to use?

Student: I use change maybe I could use . . . Opportunity.

Student: I could think of other words for *think*. I know I will use that word.

Teacher: Okay, this is a beginning. I want you to think about your
           message first. Then if you believe you are using the same word
           over and over try to change it to another similar word.

The teacher looks over students as they write. He finds it hard not to
go next to them to provide support. However, he knows he cannot do this
during the writing assessment. Following is the essay that Sandra wrote to
this prompt:

> I am going to tell you what I would like to change in the world. I would
> like to change the life of people who suffer starving. The people with
> no homes with no food. When I see a person that is homeless and has
> no food I fell like I should give him some food, and if I could I would
> give that person a place to live. What I would like to change about the
> homeless people with no food is make them live a better life.
>
> My feelings for the homeless with no food are the following. I feel like
> the back of my heart is being stabbed. My feelings fro the homeless
> with no food is that when I see a person like that I feel like I need to
> do something not just stand their and watch him or her suffer. When
> I go to the store or to an incredible place that I like and see a home-
> less person, I feel like I'm going to burst into tears forever because
> I feel terrible.
>
> Some people may not care about homeless people with no food, but
> I do. I would do anything to make them not suffer anymore. [no
> corrections]

Similar to Brooke's teacher, Sandra's teacher wrote comments to her
about this essay. This is what he wrote:

> Sandra, I can tell that you care about homeless people. Your feelings
> came through. You even gave me a picture of your feelings when you
> wrote, "like the back of my heart is being stabbed." And I love that
> you took chances with the word *incredible*. Now I want you to think
> about just one thing. In this essay you were to talk about how you
> might change the world. So on a piece of paper think about the home-
> less and what could be done to help them. You don't have to do it
> alone; you can suggest others that could help you. Remember, they
> were asking what you would do to change the world.

In this reply, Sandra's teacher compliments Sandra on important qualities of her writing such as sharing her feelings and attempts at interesting words. His suggestions guide her to the central expectations for this essay and ask her to jot down ideas she might have included. His recommendation to write about possible activities she might do to help the homeless allowed her to ponder what they might be. This activity provided her practice in carefully responding to the prompt's expectations—practice that will help her on other prompts and the state assessment.

FINAL THOUGHTS

This chapter focused on oral and written conversations centered on writing. The goal of the conversations was to build students' skill and confidence when writing. The teachers in these examples, for the most part, carefully crafted what they said to students. They knew that students needed to focus on the meaning aspects of writing to improve, and they constantly fought against giving lower-level responses centered on conventions. They also dealt with the tension of providing explicit help with writing and/or nudging students to make these discoveries with their indirect support. While they were aware that the simplest strategy was to take control of a student's writing, they supported students in seeking their own words to clarify confusions in writing, for example. In addition, they scaffolded revision for students by having them focus on one element at a time. For example, Ryan focused on adding important details before he worked on the ending to his paper.

While there are numerous ways to help students as they write, we value a simple planning sheet that asks students to think about

- What kind of writing are they doing? Narrative, informational, persuasive, poetry, and so on.
- What are the expectations for this kind of writing?
- Who are they writing for?
- Why do they think this piece of writing is important?
- What must they include?
- How will they end their writing?

These responses, then, focus conversations that teachers have with students about writing. They allow the student, in most cases, to set the purpose and audience for their writing. (This would not be true for high-stakes writing assignments.) Moreover, they serve as a guide for the teacher in having productive conferences with students—conferences that nudge students to more accomplished writing.

Afterword

We have come a considerable distance in writing instruction in the last 100 years, when writing teachers were happy to have their sixth-grade students master the skills of composing five simple error-free sentences and learn the correct form for a business letter before they left school forever to join the working world. We now have greater expectations for our students, and they have more pressing needs and reasons to become proficient writers.

In the first half of the 20th century, educators were urged to concentrate on oral language skills in the grammar grades, as K–6 grade levels were then called, since verbal skills would be the most utilized in students' future vocational and personal lives, with the exception of a very few who might become authors or journalists. Language arts textbooks spent a considerable number of pages in providing *memory gems* such as Emerson's *The Mountain and the Squirrel* or just about anything by Longfellow for students to memorize and practice pronouncing or copying onto lined pages to demonstrate mastery of the elementary English curriculum.

However, today the greater importance of oral versus written skills is no longer necessarily as true as it once was. With the advent of electronic communications, the ability to write quickly, clearly, and succinctly has assumed greater importance. Since good readers are able to process information considerably faster than most listeners can, writing has become the preferred mode of delivering informational messages in many cases. In addition, the written format supplies a record of the information to reference for future purposes.

More than ever, students and adults are relying on writing to inform, describe, convince, and entertain others. Writing as a way of thinking through issues and solving problems has become a cross-curricular tool applied throughout the content areas, as is evidenced in national standards in English or language arts, math, science, and social studies. In addition, the use of writing to measure proficiency in other content areas has enhanced its importance as well. As Richard Sterling (National Writing Project &

Nagin, 2003), director of the National Writing Project, has stated, "Today, there is an urgency to reconsider the relationship of writing to learning as well as the place of writing in our schools as we make every effort to meet our students' needs in the information age and prepare them to become informed and active citizens in the 21st century" (p. x).

Writing development is more than learning a set of discrete skills. It, like the other complex aspects of literacy, is a social process determined by contexts and cultures as well as purposes. It is a process of inquiry and a series of choices, choices that determine both thoughts and actions and a pathway to future beliefs and behaviors.

> The way we teach writing behavior, whether we will it or not, causes reverberations in all features of a student's private and social behavior. . . . In teaching students about the way they ought to use language we are teaching them something about how to conduct their lives. (Berlin, 1984, p. 92)

Appendix

WRITING PROMPTS FOR DIVERGENT WRITING TASKS (NARRATIVE, EXPOSITORY, AND PERSUASIVE)

Third- to Fourth-Grade Narrative

Everyone is surprised at one time or another. Tell a story about a time when you were surprised.

Third- to Fourth-Grade Expository

There are many amazing things in our world. Explain something you know about that is amazing.

Third- to Fourth-Grade Persuasive

Many people like to travel. Persuade someone about the best place to visit and why.

Fifth- to Sixth-Grade Narrative

Not all education takes place in school. Write about a time you learned something when you were someplace other than in school.

Fifth- to Sixth-Grade Expository

Think of an object that you value very much. Explain what that object is and why it is important to you.

Fifth- to Sixth-Grade Persuasive

You and a friend have collected $3.50 by recycling. Now the two of you are going to buy a treat to share. You each want an item that costs exactly $3.25. Decide what your treat might be and persuade your friend to purchase your choice.

Seventh- to Eighth-Grade Narrative

Think about something you do well and like to do. Tell a story about a time when you did something well that you enjoy.

Seventh- to Eighth-Grade Expository

Choose an environmental problem. Explain its importance and provide some possible solutions to it.

Seventh- to Eighth-Grade Persuasive

There is a school board meeting tonight and they are worried about low testing results. They are considering retaining all seventh and eighth graders until they can pass the test. Persuade the school board that optional Saturday school should be funded and would be a better alternative.

WRITING PROMPTS FOR CONVERGENT WRITING TASKS (READING, MATH, SCIENCE, AND SOCIAL STUDIES)

Third- to Fourth-Grade Reading

In your own words, explain the main idea of the story you just read.

Third- to Fourth-Grade Math

Some numbers in a skip-counting number pattern are shown below. The same number is added each time to get the next number. Which two numbers are missing numbers in the pattern? Explain how you arrived at your answer.

17, 21, 25, __, __, 37, 41, . . .

Third- to Fourth-Grade Science

Explain why scientists who are experimenting with flowering plants would want some insects in their garden.

Third- to Fourth-Grade Social Studies

Explain at least three reasons why we need the rules and laws of government.

Fifth- to Sixth-Grade Reading

Using two or more details from the passage you just read, tell what the main character learns during the story.

Fifth- to Sixth-Grade Math

The new school lunch menu is offering pizza topping choices. The choices are combinations of any of the following: pepperoni, sausage, mushroom, or salami. How many possible combination choices for pizza does a student have? List all the possible choices and show how you arrived at your answer.

Fifth- to Sixth-Grade Science

The beak of a bird is adapted to different feeding habits. Choose at least three different styles of bird beaks, describe them, and explain how they are best suited to particular feeding habits.

Fifth- to Sixth-Grade Social Studies

Draw an example of a peninsula and explain its characteristic features.

Seventh- to Eighth-Grade Reading

In the passage you just read, the two characters had different perspectives on their adventure. Using details from the passage, explain each of the character's perspectives and how each conflicted with the other character's point of view.

Seventh- to Eighth-Grade Math

In a game played by flipping two coins, Pete gets a point if both coins show the same side; Ashley gets a point if different sides are showing on each of the coins. Who is more likely to win after 50 tosses? Show your work and explain which person you chose as the most likely winner and why.

Seventh- to Eighth-Grade Science

The human body has several specialized systems, including the respiratory system. Name three components or organs that make up the respiratory system and describe their functions.

Seventh- to Eighth-Grade Social Studies

Identify three major shifts in the immigration patterns into the United States from the mid-19th century to the close of the 20th century. Explain at least two causes for one of the changes you have identified.

References

PREFACE

Graves, D. (2004). What I've learned from teachers of writing. *Language Arts, 82,* 88–94.

1

Atwell, N. (1998). *In the middle: New understandings about writing, reading, and learning* (2nd ed.). Portsmouth, NH: Heinemann.

Beck, I. L., Perfetti, C. A., & McKeown, M. G. (1982). Effects of long-term vocabulary instruction on lexical access and reading comprehension. *Journal of Educational Psychology, 74*(4), 506–521.

Berninger, V. W., Abbott, R. D., Abbott, S. P., Graham, S., & Richards, T. (2002). Writing and reading: Connections between language by hand and language by eye. *Journal of Learning Disabilities, 35*(1), 39–56.

Calkins, L. M. (1994). *The art of teaching writing.* Portsmouth, NH: Heinemann.

Coulmas, F. (1989). *The writing systems of the world.* New York: Blackwell.

Davis, S. J., & Winek, J. (1989). Improving expository writing by increasing background knowledge. *Journal of Reading, 33*(3), 178–181.

Graves, D. (1994). *A fresh look at writing.* Portsmouth, NH: Heinemann.

Graves, D. (2004). *Teaching day by day: 180 stories to help you along the way.* Portsmouth, NH: Heinemann.

Hayes, D. A., & Tierney, R. J. (1982). Developing readers' knowledge through analogy. *Reading Research Quarterly, 17*(2), 256–280.

Hughes, R. D. (1998). Falling off the skateboard: Experimenting with peer conferences. In R. Bullock (Ed.), *Why workshop? Changing course in 7–12 English* (pp. 78–89). Portland, ME: Stenhouse.

Levin, J. R., & Pressley, M. (1981). Improving children's prose comprehension: Selected strategies that seem to succeed. In C. M. Santa & B. L. Hayes (Eds.), *Children's prose comprehension: Research practice* (pp. 44–71). Newark, DE: International Reading Association.

Loban, W. (1963). *The language of elementary school children: A study of the use and control of language and the relations among speaking, reading, writing, and listening*

(NCTE Research Report No. 1). Champaign, IL: National Council of Teachers of English.

Moffett, J., & Wagner, B. J. (1992). *Student-centered language arts, K–12* (4th ed.). Portsmouth, NH: Boynton/Cook.

O'Donnell, R. C., Griffin, W. J., & Norris, R. C. (1967). *Syntax of kindergarten and elementary school children: A transformational analysis* (NCTE Research Report No. 8). Champaign, IL: National Council of Teachers of English.

Rumelhart, D. E. (1980). Schemata: The building blocks of cognition. In R. J. Spiro, B. C. Bruce, & W. F. Brewer, (Eds.), *Theoretical issues in reading comprehension: Perspectives from cognitive psychology, linguistics, artificial intelligence, and education* (pp. 33–58). Hillsdale, NJ: Lawrence Erlbaum.

Tchudi, S. J., & Tchudi, S. (1999). *The English language arts handbook* (2nd ed.). Portsmouth, NH: Boynton/Cook.

2

Armbruster, B. (2000). Responding to informational prose. In R. Indrisano & J. Squire (Eds.), *Perspectives on writing: Research, theory, and practice* (pp. 140–161). Newark, DE: International Reading Association.

Bear, D., Invernizzi, M., Templeton, S., & Johnston, F. (2000). *Words their way: Word study for phonics, vocabulary, and spelling instruction.* Upper Saddle River, NJ: Prentice Hall.

Britton, J. (1970). *Language and learning.* Harmondsworth, Middlesex, UK: Penguin.

Capeci, A. (2000). *The giant germ.* New York: Scholastic.

Casbergue, R., & Plauche, M. (2003). Immersing children in nonfiction: Fostering emergent research and writing. In D. Barone & L. Morrow (Eds.), *Literacy and young children: Research-based practices* (pp. 243–260). New York: Guilford.

Duke, N., Bennett-Armistead, S., & Roberts, E. (2003). Bridging the gap between learning to read and reading to learn. In D. Barone & L. Morrow (Eds.), *Literacy and young children: Research-based practices* (pp. 226–242). New York: Guilford.

Guthrie, J., Van Meter, P., McCann, A., Wigfield, A., Bennett, L., Poundstone, C., et al. (1996). Growth of literacy engagement: Changes in motivations and strategies during Concept-Oriented Reading Instruction. *Reading Research Quarterly, 31,* 306–332.

Jeunesse, G., & deBourgoing, P. (1989). *Fruit.* New York: Scholastic.

Marcchetti, V. (2001). *Orangutans.* Bothell, WA: Wright Group.

Morley, J. (1995). *How would you survive as an ancient Egyptian?* New York: Franklin Watts.

Spivey, N. (1990). Transforming texts: Constructive processes in reading and writing. *Written Communication, 7,* 256–287.

Stanley, D. (2000). *Michelangelo.* New York: HarperCollins.

Vacca, R., & Vacca, J. (2000). Writing across the curriculum. In R. Indrisano & J. Squire (Eds.), *Perspectives on writing: Research, theory, and practice* (pp. 214–232). Newark, DE: International Reading Association.

3

Atwell, N. (2002). *Lessons that change writers.* Portsmouth, NH: Heinemann.

Barone, D. (1990). The written responses of young children: Beyond comprehension to story understanding. *New Advocate, 3*(1), 49–56.

Barone, D., & Lovell, J. (1987). Bryan the brave: A second grader's growth as reader and writer. *Language Arts, 64*(5), 505–515.

Bear, D., Invernizzi, M., Templeton, S., & Johnston, F. (2000). *Words their way: Word study foe phonics, vocabulary, and spelling instruction.* Englewood Cliffs, NJ: Prentice Hall.

Bereiter, C., & Scardamalia, M. (Eds.). (1987). *The psychology of written composition.* Mahwah, NJ: Lawrence Erlbaum.

Calkins, L. (1986). *The art of teaching writing.* Portsmouth, NH: Heinemann.

Calkins, L. (1994). *The art of teaching writing* (2nd ed.). Portsmouth, NH: Heinemann.

Dyson, A. (1995). Writing children: Reinventing the development of childhood literacy. *Written Communication, 12,* 4–46.

Dyson, A. (1996). Cultural constellations and childhood identities: On Greek gods, cartoon heroes, and the social lives of school children. *Harvard Educational Review, 66,* 471–495.

Dyson, A. (1997). *Writing superheroes: Contemporary childhood, popular culture, and classroom literacy.* New York: Teachers College Press.

Dyson, A. (1999). Coach Bombay's kids learn to write: Children's appropriation of media material for school literacy. *Research in the Teaching of English, 33,* 367–402.

Dyson, A. (2001). Where are the childhoods in childhood literacy? An exploration in outer (school) space. *Journal of Early Childhood Literacy, 1,* 9–40.

Dyson, A. (2003). *The brothers and sisters learn to write: Popular literacies in childhood and school cultures.* New York: Teachers College Press.

Ferreiro, E., & Teberosky, A. (1982). *Literacy before schooling.* Portsmouth, NH: Heinemann.

Gilbert, P. (1989). *Gender, literacy, and the classroom.* Melbourne: Australian Reading Association.

Graves, D. (1983). *Writing: Teachers and children at work.* Portsmouth, NH: Heinemann.

Graves, D. (1994). *A fresh look at writing.* Portsmouth, NH: Heinemann.

Harste, J., Woodward, V., & Burke, C. (1984). *Language stories and literacy lessons.* Portsmouth, NH: Heinemann.

Jarrell, R. (1978). *A bat is born.* New York: Doubleday.

Labbo, L. (1996). Beyond storytime: A sociopsychological perspective on young children's opportunities for literacy development during story extension time. *Journal of Literacy Research, 28,* 405–428.

Martlew, M., & Sorsby, A. (1995). The precursors of writing: Graphic representation in preschool children. *Learning and Instruction, 5,* 1–19.

Millard, E. (1995). Free choice writing in the early years. *Australian Journal of Early Childhood, 20,* 33–37.

Minns, H. (1991). *Language, literacy, and gender.* London: Hodder & Stoughton.

Morris, D. (1983). Concept of word and phoneme awareness in the beginning reader. *Research in the Teaching of English, 17,* 359–373.

Murray, D. (1990). *Read to write*. Fort Worth, TX: Holt, Rinehart, & Winston.

Romano, T. (2000). *Blending genre, altering style: Writing multigenre papers*. Portsmouth, NH: Boynton/Cook.

Rowe, D. (1994). *Preschoolers as authors: Literacy learning in the social world of the classroom*. Creskill, NJ: Hampton Press.

Staton, J. (1980). Writing and counseling: Using a dialogue journal. *Language Arts, 57*, 514–518.

Synder, Z. (1967). *The Egypt game*. New York: Dell.

Tchudi, S., & Tchudi, S. (1984). *The young writer's handbook: A practical guide for the beginner who is serious about writing*. New York: Scribner.

Tompkins, G. (1990). *Teaching writing: Balancing process and product*. Columbus, OH: Merrill.

White, J. (1986). The writing on the wall: Beginning or end of a girl's career. *Women's Studies International Forum, 9*, 561–574.

Wilson, J. (1988). *Oh, brother!* New York: Scholastic.

4

Ahlberg, A. (2001). *The jolly postman*. New York: Little, Brown.

Andrade, H. G., & Boulay, B. A. (2003). Role of rubric-referenced self-assessment in learning to write. *Journal of Educational Research, 97*(1), 21–34.

Atwell, N. (1998). *In the middle: New understandings about writing, reading, and learning*. Portsmouth, NH: Boynton/Cook.

Bangert-Drowns, R. L., Hurley, M. M., & Wilkinson, B. (2004). The effects of school-based writing-to-learn interventions on academic achievement: A meta-analysis. *Review of Educational Research, 74*(1), 29–58.

Britton, J., Burgess, T., Martin, N., McLeod, A., & Rosen, H. (1975). *The development of writing abilities (11–18)*. London: Macmillan.

Chambliss, M. J., Christenson, L. A., & Parker, C. (2003). Fourth graders composing scientific explanations about the effects of pollutants: Writing to understand. *Written Communication, 20*(4), 426–454.

Dodgson, C. (n.d.). *Eight or nine wise words about letter writing: 3. How to go on with a letter*. Retrieved November 28, 2003, from http://www.hoboes.com/html/FireBlade/Carroll/Words/Letters3.html.

Elbow, P. (1973). *Writing without teachers*. New York: Oxford University Press.

Franklin, B. (1927). *Proposals for the education of youth in Pennsylvania*. Cambridge, MA: Harvard University Press. (Original work published 1749).

Glasswell, K. (1999). *The patterning of difference: Teachers and children constructing development in writing*. Unpublished doctoral dissertation, University of Auckland, Auckland, New Zealand.

Graves, D. (1978). *Balance the basics: Let them write*. New York: Ford Foundation.

Kendal, O., & Johnson, J. (1819). *Juvenile Gazette, 1*(1). Providence RI: Kendal & Johnson.

Lane, B. (1993). *After the end: Teaching and learning creative revision*. Portsmouth, NH: Heinemann.

Lanham, D. D. (2001). Writing instruction from late antiquity to the twelfth century. In J. J. Murphy (Ed.), *A short history of writing instruction* (2nd ed., pp. 79–121). Mahwah, NJ: Lawrence Erlbaum.

Newkirk, T. (2002). *Misreading masculinity: Boys, literacy, and popular culture.* Portsmouth, NH: Heinemann.

Romano, T. (1995). Writing with passion*: Life stories, multiple genres.* Portsmouth, NH: Boynton/Cook Heinemann.

Rosenshine, B., Meister, C., & Chapman, S. (1996). Teaching students to generate questions: A review of the intervention studies. *Review of Educational Research, 66*(2), 181–221.

Scieszka, J. (1992). *The true story of the 3 little pigs by A. Wolf; as told to Jon Scieszka.* New York: Viking Kestrel.

Wiesner, P. (2001). *The three pigs.* New York: Clarion Books.

5

Applebee, A. N. (1994). English language arts assessment: Lessons from the past. *English Journal, 83*(4), 40–46.

Atwell, N. (1987). *In the middle: Writing, reading, and learning with adolescents.* Portsmouth, NH: Boynton/Cook.

Ballou, F. W. (1916). Improving instruction through educational measurement. *Educational Administration & Supervision, 2*(6), 354–367.

Breed, F. S., & Frostic, F. W. (1917). A scale for measuring the general merit of English composition in the sixth grade. *Elementary School Journal, 17*(5), 307–325.

Butler, V. M. (1969). *Education as revealed by New England newspapers prior to 1850.* New York: Arno Press & The New York Times. (Reprinted from dissertation of the same title, Temple University, 1935, Teachers College Library.) (Original work published 1935).

Caldwell, O. W., & Courtis, S. A. (1971). *Then & now in education 1845–1923: A message of encouragement from the past to the present.* New York: Arno Press & The New York Times. (Original work published 1925).

Cooper, M. M. (1997). Communicating with parents and the public. In S. Tchudi (Ed.), *Alternatives to grading student writing* (pp. 301–305). Urbana, IL: National Council of Teachers of English.

Duke, N. K. (2004). The case for informational text. *Educational Leader, 61*(6), 40–44.

Fagan, W. T., Cooper, C. R., & Jensen, J. M. (1975). *Measures for research and evaluation in the English language arts.* Urbana, IL: ERIC Clearinghouse on Reading and Communication Skills and National Council of Teachers of English.

Freedman, S. W. (1993). Linking large-scale testing and classroom portfolio assessments of student writing. *Educational Assessment, 1,* 27–52.

Hillocks, G., Jr. (2002). *The testing trap: How state writing assessment controls learning.* New York: Teachers College Press.

Hosic, J. F. (1929). Editorial: Methods in creative writing. *English Journal, 18*(4), 345–346.

Hudelson, E. (1923). English composition: Its aims, methods, and measurement. In G. W. Whipple (Ed.), *Part I, The Twenty-Second Yearbook, National Society for the Study of Education* (pp. 1–172). Bloomington, IL: Public School Publishing.

Lathe, A. M. (1889). Written examinations: Their abuse, and their use. *Education, 9*(7), 452–456.

Leonard, S. A. (1925). Building a scale of purely composition quality. *English Journal, 14*(10), 760–775.

Lloyd-Jones, R. (1977). Primary trait scoring. In C. R. Cooper & L. Odell (Eds.), *Evaluating writing: Describing, measuring, judging* (pp. 33–66). Urbana, IL: National Council of Teachers of English.

Lyman, R. L. (1929). *Summary of investigations relating to grammar, language, and composition.* Chicago: University of Chicago Press.

Mayher, J. S. (1990). *Uncommon sense: Theoretical practice in language education.* Portsmouth, NH: Boynton/Cook.

Murray, L. (1825). *English grammar. Adapted to the different classes of learners with an appendix containing rules and observations for assisting the more advanced students to write with perspicuity and accuracy* (9th ed.). Boston: T. Bedlington. (Original work published 1795).

National Council of Teachers of English. (1995). *Writing assessment: A position statement.* Retrieved November 16, 2004, from http://www.ncte.org/about/over/positions/category/assess/107610.htm.

Portalupi, J., & Fletcher, R. (2004). *Teaching the qualities of writing.* Portsmouth, NH: Firsthand.

Spandel, V., & Culham, R. (1994). *Picture books: An annotated bibliography for use with the 6-trait analytic model of writing assessment and instruction* (2nd ed.). Portland, OR: Northwest Regional Lab.

Stotsky, S. (1995). The uses and limitations of personal or personalized writing in writing theory, research, and instruction. *Reading Research Quarterly 30,* 758–776.

Tompkins, G. E. (2004). *Teaching writing: Balancing process and product* (4th ed.). Upper Saddle River, NJ: Pearson Education.

Trabue, M. R. (1917). Supplementing the Hillegas scale. *Teachers College Record, 18*(1), 51–84.

Van Wagenen, M. J. (1921). The Minnesota English composition scales: Their derivation and validity. *Educational Administration and Supervision, 7*(9), 481–499.

White, E. M. (1985). *Teaching and assessing writing.* San Francisco: Jossey-Bass.

White, E. M. (1994). *Teaching and assessing writing: Recent advances in understanding evaluating, and improving student performance* (2nd ed.). San Francisco: Jossey-Bass.

Willing, M. H. (1918). The measurement of written composition in grades IV to VIII. *English Journal, 7*(3), 193–202.

Wolcott, W., & Legg, S. M. (1998). *An overview of writing assessment: Theory, research, and practice.* Urbana, IL: National Council of Teachers of English.

6

Benard, B. (2004). *Resiliency: What we have learned.* San Francisco: WestEd.

Calkins, L. (1994). *The art of teaching writing* (2nd ed.). Portsmouth, NH: Heinemann.

Dyson, A. (1999). Coach Bombay's kids learn to write: Children's appropriation of media material for school literacy. *Research in the Teaching of English, 33,* 367–402.

Johnston, P. (2004). *Choice words: How our language affects children's learning.* Portland, ME: Stenhouse.

Konigsburg, E. (1967). *From the mixed-up files of Mrs. Basil E. Frankweiler.* New York: Dell.

Paley, V. (1981). *Wally stories: Conversations in kindergarten*. Cambridge, MA: Harvard University Press.

Tompkins, G. (2004). *Teaching writing: Balancing process and product* (4th ed.). Upper Saddle River, NJ: Pearson.

AFTERWORD

Berlin, J. A. (1984). *Writing instruction in nineteenth-century American colleges*. Carbondale: Southern Illinois University Press.

National Writing Project & Nagin, C. (2003). *Because writing matters: Improving student writing in our schools*. San Francisco: Jossey-Bass.

Index

**CORWIN
PRESS**

The Corwin Press logo—a raven striding across an open book—represents the union of courage and learning. Corwin Press is committed to improving education for all learners by publishing books and other professional development resources for those serving the field of PreK–12 education. By providing practical, hands-on materials, Corwin Press continues to carry out the promise of its motto: **"Helping Educators Do Their Work Better."**